THE COMPLETE BOOK OF CREATIVE GLASS ART

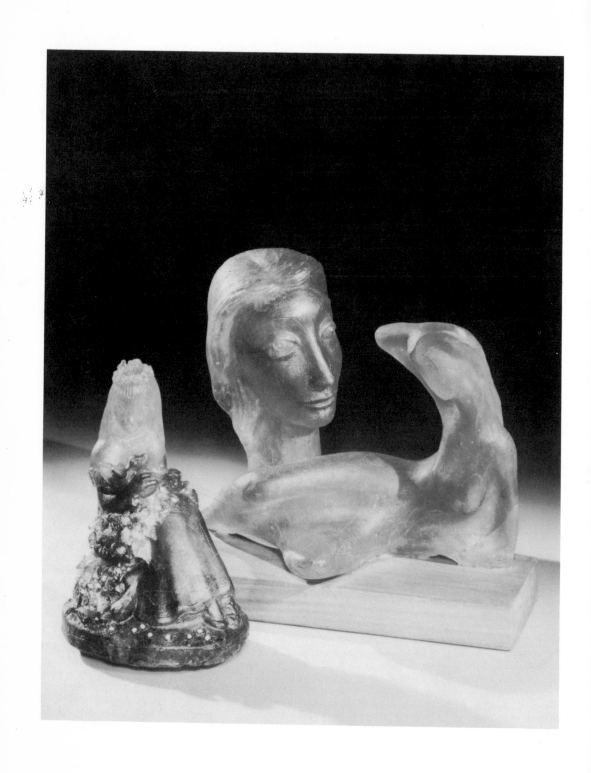

THE COMPLETE BOOK OF CREATIVE GLASS ART

by Polly Rothenberg

CROWN PUBLISHERS, INC., NEW YORK

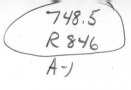
Also by the Author

METAL ENAMELING
THE COMPLETE BOOK OF CERAMIC ART
CREATIVE STAINED GLASS

Acknowledgments

I AM indebted to the talented and friendly individual glass artists and members of professional glass studios who have contributed the photographs of their inspired works that appear in this book. Many of them have attained an impressive standing in their special fields. I sincerely thank Helene Weis of the Willet Stained Glass Studios for her courteous assistance in supplying fine process photos of members of the studio's large staff of talented and skilled artists at work on actual projects.

Thanks also go to the staff of *Ceramics Monthly* for permission to include in the book material of mine that has appeared in their publication. My appreciation is extended to the Toledo Museum of Art for allowing me to select photographs from the "American Glass Now" exhibition for the section of the book relating to contemporary glassblowing. And Bob Brodecki of Etmans Lab thank you again for your fine custom prints made from my negatives.

My deep appreciation goes to Vernon Brejcha who generously demonstrated for the book photo-sequences of his glassblowing specialties and to Sherry Brejcha who captured the essence of the action with her camera.

I especially thank again all the fine and friendly folks at the Georgian College of Applied Arts and Technology in Barrie, Ontario, for the courtesies extended me during the time I spent in their Glass Design Department summer workshop. Roman Bartkiw's watchful guidance through the basics of glassblowing made it possible for me to have some experience in this fascinating art. Sandblasting, etching, and engraving, as well as other "cold glass" techniques made the workshop a rewarding experience. My thanks go to Georgian College staff members Wayne Cunningham, David Phillips, Jack Hunt, and Charles McManus. Marc Robillard's stunning photographs of Roman Bartkiw "blocking" a blown glass bubble with a wet newspaper and photos of other activities in the glass department are valuable additions to the book. Finally, I sincerely thank my husband, Maurice, for his patient and helpful cooperation in this project.

Contents

4 FIRED GLASS

5 DECORATING METHODS AND PROJECTS

6 GLASS JEWELRY

7 BLOWN GLASS

8 GLASS SCULPTURE AND ARCHITECTURAL ART

Preface

GLASS art has been endowed with mystery and glamor since the prehistoric days when the first shining beads were molded from silica sand, potash, and lime. Although archaeologists have unearthed crude glass objects in Egypt that presumably were made over 3,000 years ago, there is evidence among the findings that many of the older glass articles uncovered came from Asia. Discoveries also reveal that during those early years, glass in the form of jewelry and small statues was owned by the wealthy and the noble. Glassmakers were under strict supervision of the ruling Pharaohs. To the common people, glass was mysterious, glamorous, and unattainable.

Until the advent of the blown glass bubble, colored beads, small amulets, and statues were the most cherished glass forms, not only for personal adornment and pleasure but also for use as trade currency and tax payments. The discovery, just prior to the Christian era, that glass can be blown was a major achievement. As time passed and glass became more plentiful, Phoenician traders carried it throughout the Mediterranean area. Glass beads became available to others besides the wealthy and high-born. But across the Mediterranean a newer, more imperious empire was stirring. Eventually Egyptian power and pre-eminence in glassmaking fell to the Romans. By the beginning of the Christian era, the Roman Emperor Tiberius had transported captive Egyptian glassworkers to Rome and had settled them there and in his vassal colonies over Europe wherever sand and fuel were available. He was so enamored with glass that it is said he even learned how to make it himself.

The first four centuries of the Christian era became the first golden age of glass. Glassblowing created a thin wall that could be seen through, an amazing accomplishment to the ordinary Roman citizen who attributed strange powers to the master glassmakers. The Romans began to experiment in earnest to produce thinner, clearer glass. They decorated this fragile, clear glass with applied colored glass threads, painted it with gilt and enamel, added "prunts," or pressed lumps of molten glass, and used many of the methods contemporary glass craftsmen employ today to enrich the surface of their blown forms. But with the rise and fall of the Roman Empire, the development of glass rose and fell also. A succession of powerful barbarian tribes from the north overpowered and pillaged the western Mediterranean. During the next four hundred years, Roman glory and the first golden age of glass grew dim.

The savage hordes that ravaged Europe left destruction and decay. But the secrets of glassmaking did not perish. Constantinople became more than a caretaker political and cultural power for all the Mediterranean world. Glass mosaic-making flourished in Byzantium. By the twelfth century, Christian missionaries emigrating from Constantinople established monasteries all over Europe and glassmaking was one of their important arts.

As the years passed, the City of Venice was destined to replace Constantinople as the center of the glass arts. Founded in the sixth century by refugees from the plunderers of Rome, the marshy islands of sand where they achieved safety proved to be ideal for making glass. Beech forests nearby just across the Gulf of Venice yielded the fuel and potash. With these advantages, Venice needed only to acquire the techniques of glassmaking; she brought in master glassworkers from her captured colony of Syria. The secrecy of Venetian glassmaking techniques and the intrigue surrounding glass art became legendary. By the end of the thirteenth century, to protect their glass secrets, Venetian authorities had moved all their glassworkers to the small offshore island of Murano. Their movements were closely restricted, although from time to time freedom-loving Venetians managed to slip away. But again glassmaking was shrouded in mystery.

With the spread of Christianity, glass mosaics had become a major art. But a newer form in colored glass was emerging. A development in religious architecture, the Gothic cluster of arches with their supporting columns, niches and spaces between them, became ideal for cloistering colored glass windows. Wealthy nobility supplied the materials with which artisan monks were to design and construct them. The twelfth and thirteenth centuries became the second golden age of glass. Glass art in all its forms developed and flourished as never before or since that time until the twentieth century. Some of the mystery of glass has lessened, but man's ability to create new forms with this exciting material has scarcely begun.

This book concerns the glass art of our time, its craftsmen, and the many ways it is formed. Now more than ever, people with leisure to enjoy all the arts yearn to create decorative works that are uniquely their own. Anyone who loves beauty can learn how to make decorative glass objects by following easily understood but precise directions. The illustrated and detailed step-by-step instructions in the book offer both simple and complex projects that are exciting to follow. As your skill develops, your own confidence and creativity will emerge. Once you have conquered the processes, you can develop unusual and creative ideas of your own. Throughout these pages there are beautiful photographs of the works of skilled and talented professional glass artists, illustrating the amazing variety of their styles. Their works will be an inspiration to experienced craftsmen, to collectors, and to those who are just discovering the joyful world of glass.

1
Introduction

STAINED GLASS

FOR centuries stained glass has richly adorned the churches of the world, uplifting the spirits of millions of worshipers. Except for brief historical interludes when stained glass was used in private dwellings, it was associated almost entirely with religious architecture. Today, the classical art of designing with this beautiful transparent material has swept aside the last restraints of its ancient role. Although it is still very important in religious architecture, stained glass has moved into the modern world of secular construction and home workshop creations. With new attitudes and new ways of utilizing the vibrant beauty of its colors, enthusiastic craftsmen are creating delightful glass panels, windows, beautiful lanterns, jewelry, whimsical hangings, sculptures, and countless accessories.

Stained glass as an artistic creation depends for its beauty on the transmitted light that illuminates it from moment to moment.

Moving daylight sends its rays through each bit of glass in ever-changing hues. Simple shapes become alive the moment they capture a gleam of sunshine. The origin and force of the light are phenomena that form the basis of stained glass designing. Not only must the glass artist reckon with light coming through the glass, but also with the changing color effects of whatever is seen beyond the glass. These modulating elements may themselves be in full sunlight, in shadow, or dappled with light and shadow. All these effects are heightened by the texture and undulations in the stained glass itself.

COLOR IN GLASS

Light moving through vibrant stained glass is influenced by many factors: the time of day; the types and sources of lighting; highlights and shadows; the effects of halation due to the juxtaposition of certain colors; the transparency, texture, and luminosity of the glass itself

◄

Bonded exhibition panel. Louis Moses. A prismatic display of stained glass color overlaid with areas of colorless glass strips set on edge to diffuse the underlying hues in third dimension. *Photo by courtesy of Willet Stained Glass Studios.*

as well as the personal interpretation of these factors. When you stand before a great stained glass window shimmering with color, your emotions will differ from those of any other person. Scientists have learned that color originates in the human brain, stimulated by light rays of varying lengths that are transmitted from objects to the eye of the beholder. Hence, color as experienced by each individual is personal and involves the mind as well as the eyes. The blue pattern one person sees may not be the same blue pattern as experienced by another.

Although no direction can be given on how to select glass colors that will satisfy all persons, it is suggested that early in the work of the serious glass art student, a good book on color should be studied, especially before important amounts of money are invested in glass. The beginner or amateur can discover beauty and emotion in color by observing nature. The subtle overtones and harmonies of translucent flower petals, butterflies, or glistening tropical fish glowing in sunlight are often enhanced by adding startling contrasts, such as bright pink spots on the pale chartreuse wings of a moth or purple splotches in the cup of a yellow tulip. Books filled with color plates of these and other natural forms are in every public library. They can yield rich and inspirational ideas to help the beginner select rewarding color combinations for his initial projects. The final selection of stained glass colors should be made by viewing them in bright natural daylight, whether you are developing an impressive stained glass wall or a decorative glass butterfly. Certain color subtleties in the glass can be discerned only by transmitted natural light. Black, which stands out so forcefully in paintings and natural forms, is overpowered by dazzling patches of light streaming through brilliant colored glass. Frequently, dark passages are desirable in a stained glass composition. But the subtle use of a dark hue already employed in the design can give more pervasive overtones to the glass composition than black glass could offer.

KINDS OF STAINED GLASS

Antique stained glass is the costliest and most exciting of the colored glasses. Spectacular stained glass church windows, panels, and windows in public and private buildings, and charming functional and decorative art objects are fashioned from this handmade glass. Despite its name it is not old glass; but it is made in nearly the same way glass was formed by early glassmakers. Skilled craftsmen employ simple tools and methods to produce hand-formed sheet glass in hundreds of new colors developed by modern chemistry. Antique glass has random streaks, ripples, undulations, bubbles, or other irregularities whose seeming imperfections catch light transmitted through them to bring character and beauty to your work. Areas of preferred thicknesses in this glass are cut and sold from larger sheets, which results in a considerable waste or "curious" glass that is sometimes sold by glass supply stores at a discount. This scrap sheet glass is useful for projects in basic glasscraft. Although it may not fit easily into a large leaded glass composition, it is suitable for bonding with epoxy resin, for grouted projects, jewelry, mobiles, and other decorative hangings.

Flashed stained glass denotes a variety of antique glass with a light colored glass base and thinner skins of rich deep contrasting colored glass. By examining the edges of a piece of flashed glass, you can see these separate color layers. Light passing through flashed glass mixes the separate color effects much the way a painter mixes his pigments. Flashed glass is useful in any project where it will not be transformed by heat: etched glass, lead came project, glass bonded with epoxy or combinations of these methods. If flashed glass is fired, the thin layer of colored glass will likely pull back from the edges, leaving a colorless or white rim around the glass piece. Flashed glass should be *cut* on the unflashed side, but it should be *etched* on the flashed side.

Cathedral glass is a machine-rolled stained glass with medium to heavy texture on one side and a smooth surface on the reverse side. It is passed between rollers that impress a variety of textures on it while the glass is still hot and pliable. Because the glass is generally of uniform thickness of ⅛ inch, there is less waste than from cutting antique glass. It is sold in a wide variety of delightful colors and textures. Rolled patterns in this glass are called hammered, rippled, seedy (containing tiny bubbles), and antique texture. Cathedral glass is cut on the smooth surface.

Slab glass (faceted glass) is the name given to an extra-clear-colored antique glass cast in thick slabs. An unusual cutting procedure called "faceting" gives them reflective sparkle and leaves a myriad of small thick glass chips, which have many decorative uses. The glass slabs are generally 8 by 8 inches, 8 by 12 inches, or 12 by 12 inches; they may vary from ½ to 1 inch in thickness. A steel wedge, a dalle cutting hammer, and special skills are required to cut these extra-thick slabs. But the novice can make wonderful projects with broken segments of this glass. Most glass suppliers sell broken slab glass segments.

Rondels are round disks of antique glass made by blowing a bubble, then twirling the hot molten glass bubble on the end of the blowing rod to flatten it by centrifugal force. Rondels are made in many sizes and beautiful colors. These very decorative forms are useful in leaded and bonded compositions.

Jewels are small novelty stained glass forms used decoratively either singly or as part of a larger composition. In addition, jewels are made by firing small glass bits into balls or cabochon shapes according to the temperature at which they are fired. They are especially effective when they are bonded on stained glass lanterns.

Opalescent glass is a milky semitranslucent glass in one or more colors and white, swirled together while the glass is still molten and finally rolled into sheets. The glass is somewhat brittle and difficult to cut.

Layered three-dimensional stained glass panel. Fredrica Fields. *Photo by Kenneth Fields.*

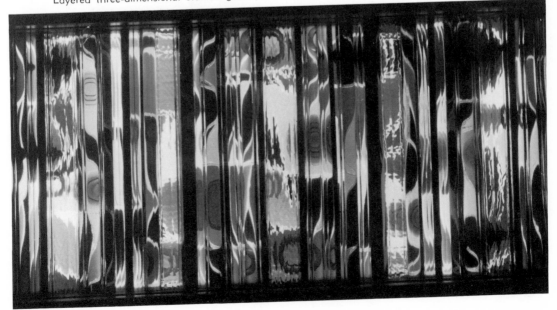

TO RAVEN. Beth Beede. Bent colorless sheet glass is mirrored and painted with black designs. Loops of wire are soldered to a lead camed edge to hold threads and fibers of Mylar. Black downy feathers are fastened into the fibers. *Photo by Erik Redlich.*

Off-hand blown bottles. Kent Ipsen. Mr. Ipsen is Chairman of the Craft Department of Virginia Commonwealth University in Richmond.

CUTTING THE GLASS

Although your first project may be confined to compositions made from glass scraps, you will find random shapes that can be improved by a little nipping and cutting here and there as you visualize how you can combine them into attractive designs. "Cutting glass" is a term that does not adequately describe the process. When glass is scored with a tiny sharp metal wheel set into a metal handle, only the surface of the glass is fractured. The cut encourages glass molecules to open up along a scored line, *when adequate pressure is applied.* This pressure must be applied at once, if you would make a clean separation. If more than a couple of minutes elapse, the separated molecules of glass will "close ranks" so that a clean separation is not achieved, even though the scored line is still visible. This characteristic of glass is unknown to the average novice. It may exlpain why a clean scored line does not always result in a clean separation of the glass when you are first learning to cut it.

Certain safety precautions must be followed when you work with glass. Always wear gloves when you transport large glass sheets. Keep glass bins on the floor so you need not elevate the glass above your head; it may have fine cracks that will make it break suddenly as you move it. If a sheet of glass begins to fall, do not grab it; step back and let it fall. If a choice piece is partly buried beneath other pieces of glass, remove the upper glass, starting from the top. If you try to shuffle the glass around with bare hands, you are likely to receive multiple gashes. Always scrape or sand the edges of newly cut glass to remove the thin sharp slivers that often appear along a freshly cut edge. The most common cause of small aggravating and painful cuts is absentmindedly brushing or pressing the bare hands on the minute glass shards that litter the cutting table's cutting surface after a session of glass cutting. If you receive a few of these painful (although usually not severe) cuts, you will automatically discontinue this careless practice. Happily, very few glass craftsmen cut themselves severely.

An inexpensive *glass cutter* with a hard steel cutting wheel is adequate for general use and it will give long service when proper care is exercised. Tungsten carbide cutting wheels, a little more expensive, give longer service and greater separation of the glass surface when it is scored. Commercial diamonds set into glass cutters are costly and they are not easy for the inexperienced craftsman to control, although many professional glass craftsmen like the flexibility they provide in cutting intricate shapes. The cutters used for projects in this book have tungsten carbide cutting wheels.

The *cutting table* must be firm, flat, and level. To maintain good arm leverage, it is advisable to stand while you cut glass. The table should have a comfortable height for this standing position. About 34 to 36 inches from the floor is adequate working table height for the average person. If the table is too low, your back will begin to feel the strain. Short-pile carpet makes a good cutting surface for the table top. Tiny slivers from glass cuttings drop into the pile where they do not interfere with subsequent cutting or scratch the glass when it is being shifted. Carpet is resilient enough to "give" under the pressure exerted to separate the scored glass. Vacuum the carpet occasionally, or if it is a very small piece shake it gently over a broad trash container to rid it of accumulated glass scraps. Some craftsmen prefer to place layers of paper or a sheet of pressed cork on the cutting table instead of carpet, especially when a limited amount of glass cutting is done.

Although rulers or other *straightedges* can guide the cutter when straight lines are scored, they have the annoying propensity of shifting suddenly or sliding on the glass (especially on uneven antique stained glass). Until you become adept at cutting glass, you can control this slippage by gluing a long strip of thin rubber to the underside of the straightedge. "Rug grip," sold in carpet stores, is excellent for this purpose. Before cutting begins, clean the glass with detergent water to remove all soil that may cause the cutter to "skip" and make separation of the scored glass difficult or ragged. Lubricate the cutting wheel with kerosene. When you score glass, hold the cutter perpendicular to the table top. It can lean slightly toward you, but if it tilts sideways one edge of the score may be undercut and make a rough separation of the glass.

Position the glass on the table *smoothest side up.* Dip the cutter into kerosene and dab it on a paper towel to remove excess oil. Beginning about ⅛ inch from the edge of the glass to avoid chipping it, make a firm continuous stroke from one edge of the glass to the other *without pausing or lifting* the cutter. Score either toward you or away from you, whichever is easier and allows you to see where you are going. Hold the cutter close to the straightedge but not pressed against it. The cutter must not wander away from the line you are scoring. Press it firmly against the glass. It should make a soft steady scratching sound as it bites into the glass but does not roughen the score line. Long straight cuts against a guide stick are not automatically easy to control; they require strict concentration. If the cutter begins to lean sideways, the cutting wheel may curve away from the straightedge. Some craftsmen prefer to lay a straightedged sheet of paper under the glass and guide the cutting wheel above it. Only experience can teach you how firmly pressure must be applied. In spite of a few false starts, it is surprising how quickly you will gain confidence after a session of practice on glass scraps or inexpensive window glass.

As soon as the glass has been scored, lay one end of your glass cutter under the near end of the score line and immediately press firmly down with your thumbs on each side of the line at the end nearest you. The scored glass should separate evenly. If it doesn't, lay the glass over the table edge so the scored line comes just beyond and parallel to the table top; with one hand pressing the glass firmly against the top of the table, snap the glass in two with the other hand bending it down and away from the table. Hang onto the glass as you force it down so it does not fall suddenly to the floor and shatter. After these two tries, if you have

not separated the glass, another procedure must be tried. Hold the glass in one hand and with the end of the cutter in the other hand, tap firmly but gently all along the scored line underneath the glass. Tap first at one end, then at the other end and along the middle of the line. You will soon see a fracture developing under the scored line. Hold the glass over the table in case it should fall apart suddenly, which it frequently will do. Apply equal pressure to the two sides of the fractured score line and snap them apart. Long curved lines are cut the same way if they are not too sharply curved. Glass thicker than ⅛ inch is difficult for beginners to cut.

To cut out a shaped piece of glass, a different method is employed. Select a pattern template and lay it on a piece of glass with at least a ¾-inch margin around the shape. With the fingers of one hand spread out on the template, hold it firmly against the glass, taking care that it does not slip while you are scoring around it. One side of the glass shape will be scored and separated at a time. Dip the cutter into kerosene and dab it lightly on a paper towel. Begin at one edge of the glass and score along one side of the pattern, continuing beyond it to the opposite edge of the glass without pausing or lifting the cutter. Lay down the cutter at once and pick up the glass before the score line heals, as described earlier; applying firm equal pressure on each side of the scored line, snap the glass down and out. If you are cutting off a thin strip of glass, grasp it on the narrow side of the score line with glass pliers or other flat end pliers and on the other side with the other hand or another pair of pliers. If you wrap narrow masking tape or a thin cloth strip around the plier's jaws, you can avoid splintering the glass when the hard metal clutches it. It may be necessary to tap sharply along the underside of the score line to *start* the fracture; then press down and out on each side of the fracture line as described for straight cuts. If you try to complete the glass separation only by tapping it until it falls apart, you will have a ragged cut. Each side of the shape is cut by scoring and separating the same way, before the next side is cut. Remember to sand its edges lightly with fine sandpaper or scrape them with another piece of glass to remove sharp border slivers. By meticulous attention to this precaution, you can avoid painful cuts.

When you have cut out the curved shape as best you can, you will likely be left with unwanted small projections along its edges. They must be chipped, or "grozed," away. Although the notches in glass cutters are meant traditionally to be used for grozing, today many craftsmen prefer to use the tips of the jaws on a pair of grozing nippers or ordinary small pliers to pinch off small projections of glass. If the thickness of the glass will fit closely into one of the notches on the cutter, with care you can successfully chip off irregularities. But if the notch is a bit wider than the thickness of the glass, the projection may take too much glass with it when it separates; you may be left with an unwanted jagged notch instead of an unwanted projection. To pinch off irregularities, grasp only the portion you want to remove from the glass edge and squeeze or pinch the nippers with quick firm pressure until you literally bite off the glass protrusion with the nipper jaws. Because the glass cutting process is fundamentally quite simple, the novice can pass from nervous frustration to easy skill in a relatively short time. Occasionally you will encounter glass bubbles and other surface irregularities when you are cutting antique stained glass. Ease the cutter over them gently without lifting it from the glass; try to avoid forcing a ragged cut through the irregularity. These bubbles and thick areas give beauty and character to the glass. After a little experience you will ride the cutter smoothly over them.

A circle cutter is required for cutting out perfect circles of glass; or you can have them cut by your local glass supplier. To cut your own, position the pivot of the cutter on a square sheet of glass, allowing about ¾ inch clearance all around. Follow exactly the instructions that accompany the circle cutter. If the cutter's rubber disk, which clamps against the glass, tends to let go of the glass while you are cutting it, wipe it with a film of water, then clamp it down again. You should have no further difficulty with it. To facilitate scoring, before you begin, hold a small brush dipped in kerosene in the hand that will swing the cutter around; lift the cutter wheel off the glass but hold the brush against it so it brushes a band of kerosene onto the glass in the path where the cutting wheel will score. Then lay the brush down and score the circle by pressing the cutting wheel against the glass as you score it in a complete circle without pausing until you hear a light click as the cutter joins the starting end of the score line. Remove the circle cutter from the glass and score four straight lines radiating out from near the circle to the edge of each side of the glass sheet. Tap gently but persistently all along the underside of the scored circle until a crack develops in it. Tap under the four radiating lines in the same way. The glass should separate easily. Hold the glass above the table and close to it while you tap so it does not fall to the floor. Regardless of how awkward you may feel initially, do not become discouraged. (Read these cutting instructions over several times until you feel ready to begin the fascinating experience of cutting glass.)

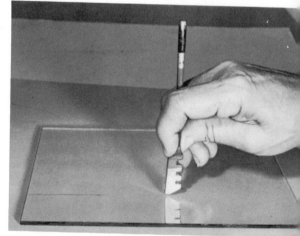

Hold the glass cutter perpendicular between your first and second fingers. The thumb supports the cutter on the underneath side of the flat surface just above the cutter notches. The tiny cutting wheel rides on the glass.

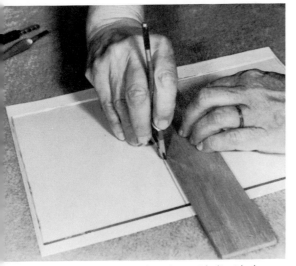

Before you start, clean the glass with liquid cleaner. Begin scoring about 1/16" from the edge of the glass and make a firm, even, continuous stroke from one edge to the other without pausing or lifting the cutter. Do not retrace the stroke. As you reach the end of the score line, relax your hand so the cutter does not chip the glass edge.

As soon as the glass has been scored, lay one end of the cutter under the near end of the score line and immediately press down firmly on each side of the line. The glass should separate evenly.

When you score straight lines along a guide stick, keep the straightedge from slipping by gluing a wide strip of thin rubber "rug grip" to the underside of the guide stick. It can be bought in rug stores.

Another method of separating the glass. With one hand pressing the glass against the table top, and with the score line extending over the edge and parallel to it, snap the glass down and out.

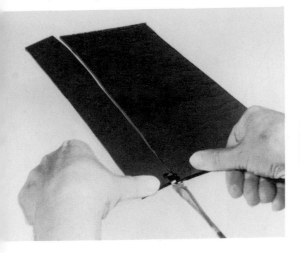

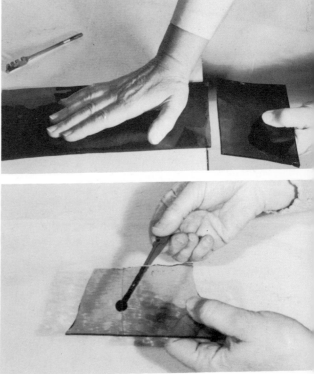

Tap firmly but gently all along the scored line underneath the glass for another way to separate it. You will see a fracture developing under the scored line.

Apply equal pressure to the two sides of the *fractured* score line and snap them apart.

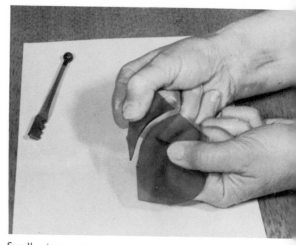

Small pieces are snapped apart on the score line with the thumbs and curled forefingers pressing down and outward.

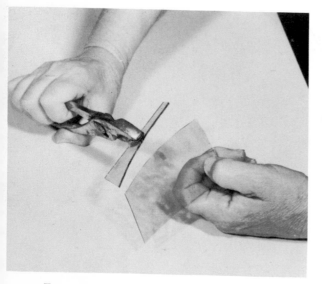

To separate a thin strip of glass from a wider section, grasp the glass on the narrow side of the score line with regular pliers or glass pliers and on the other side with your hand. Notice that the glass is always held between the thumb and curled forefinger to provide safe leverage for parting the glass.

With the fingers of one hand spread out to hold the pattern firmly against the glass, cut along the second side from edge to edge of the glass.

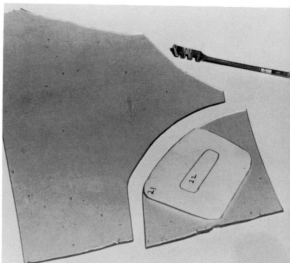

The first cut for a shaped piece is made by scoring along one side of the pattern from one edge of the glass to the other.

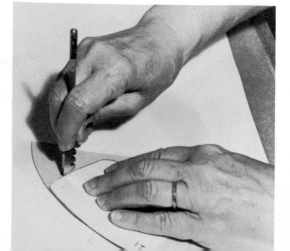

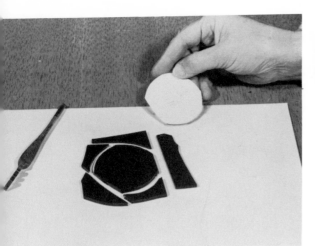

A rounded shape is cut out in a series of short curved strokes.

Corners and unwanted projections are "grozed," or nipped off, with small flat-nosed pliers or grozing pliers.

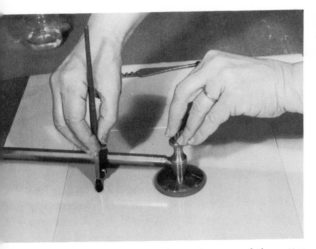

Lift the cutting wheel and swinging arm of the cutter off the glass while you hold a kerosened brush against the cutter. Scribe a full circle with the brush (not with the cutter) to put kerosene where the cutter will score the glass. Put down the brush, press the cutter against the glass, and score it on the kerosened path made by the brush.

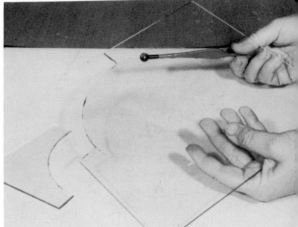

If the glass has not separated, light tapping under the score lines should complete the separation.

When the circle has separated, sand the edge lightly with wet carborundum paper.

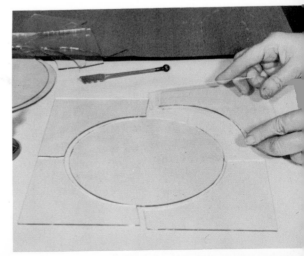

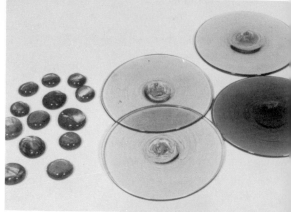

Rondels and flat marbles.

A glass storage cabinet. The top section for holding small pieces is set back to leave space for a shelf.

LEAD CAME

The slender channeled lead stripping that becomes the chief skeletal support in a leaded stained glass composition is called "lead came" (came), or just "lead." In addition to holding the glass construction together, lead came becomes a dynamic linear pictorial or abstract design with its lead lines and colorful glass being of equal importance to a successful composition. Structural strength requires that leads run vertically, horizontally, and/or diagonally, not in parallel lines alone. Avoid running several lead ends together at one point. What to do with all these ends where they meet would become an aesthetic as well as a structural problem. The lead lines are designated first on the original cartoon (drawing), then glass colors are selected.

To achieve interest and avoid monotony, lengths and widths of lead should vary. The chief structural lines of the design may be composed of heavier leads than the ones chosen to delineate delicate details, which can be worked out with narrower leads. Important lines are sweeping and rhythmical with lesser details being more subtle; they should not dart or wander aimlessly across the glass composition.

Lead widths are measured across the top surface rather than across the channeled sides. This top surface may be flat or rounded. Lead is usually available in six-foot lengths of varying styles and widths. H-shaped leads have double channels and a $\frac{1}{16}$-inch-thin wall or heart between channels. From an end view, the lead is shaped exactly like a capital H. The crossbar on the H represents the thin lead heart. H cames are employed for joining pieces of stained glass to one another within the composition and for border leads where the unused outside channel will be framed or puttied into a window. The H-leads used for the projects in this book are in the range of $\frac{1}{8}$ to $\frac{1}{4}$ inch wide, with the exception of the wider flat border leads.

U-shaped lead has one channel and is rounded or flat on the opposite side. It is intended for perimeter leading where a more finished effect is preferred. However, most professionals who usually make large compositions split a wide H-lead down through the center heart with a chisel or leading knife and bend the wide strips lengthwise to make their own U-leads if they want to use them; but this does take some skill. A $\frac{1}{8}$-inch U-lead with a flat side is a versatile and flexible lead commonly employed to finish free-form hangings or "light catchers" so dear to the hobbyist. However, the more delicate U-leads can be used in the construction of a quite professionally executed glass design. These ⅛-inch flat U-leads are employed in the construction of intricate patterns in glass lampshades to give them a sturdy but fragile-looking form.

Although the creative craftsman of today uses whatever tools he desires, whether traditional, personally designed, or improvised, the artist who devotes considerable time to stained glass work eventually acquires professional tools. A glazier's knife with a curved thin blade of top-quality steel has a thick wooden handle, useful for tapping glass pieces into the leads. Glazier's knives, lead stretchers, grozing pliers, and other glazing tools can be bought from major supply sources found in art glass publications.

Frequently, lead must be stretched and straightened before it can be used. Fasten one end of a lead strip in a vise or lead stretcher and pull firmly on the other end with pliers until you feel it stretch. Take hold of the lead with the other hand so that if it should break suddenly, you will not fall backward. If the lead is kinked or twisted, straighten and untwist it, then slide the flattened and waxed end of a dowel stick or glazier's lathekin between its flanges to open them. With a sharp knife such as a regular glazing knife or matt knife, cut the lead into usable lengths by rocking the knife from side to side through the lead. (For additional information about using lead came, see the section "Leading a Rectangular Panel.")

A set of stained glass doors. Jack A. Landis. Colors are purple, red, green, gold set against a light green hammered cathedral glass background. From the home of Mr. and Mrs. R. M. Graf, Dayton, Ohio. *Photo by Kathy Clark.*

Rounded and flat H leads have double channels. An end view shows the lead shaped like an H. A crossbar represents a thin wall, or "heart," between channels. Glass pieces fit into the channels, which hold them securely in place.

To stretch lead, fasten one end of the strip in a vise and pull firmly on the other end with pliers until you feel it stretch.

Draw the flattened end of a length of dowel stick, ¼" thick, along the lead channels to open them.

To cut lead, first score it to mark the location of the cut, then rock the knife blade gently as you press through the lead.

Lead camed stained glass panel. Herbert Tepping. The leading gives charm to a very simple statement in stained glass.

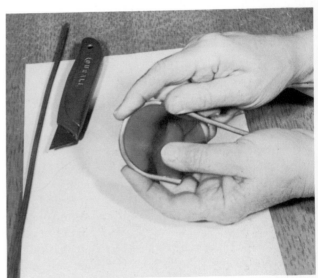

Rounded H lead is bent snugly around a curved shape without crimping it.

To trim lead ends so they form a sharp angle, hold the knife blade so it continues an imaginary line running through the center of the corner angle. The leads will form a neat juncture when they are mitered.

SOLDERING

Each separate length of lead came in a stained glass work must be soldered to adjoining pieces of lead. A 100-watt soldering iron with a copper tip and wooden handle heats up readily and is lightweight to hold. The kind of tip you use is a personal choice to some extent and may be limited to whatever is available. Examine the various soldering irons and tips at a reliable hardware store. You will find that there are three basic shapes to the tips and many variations of these: chisel, conical, and pyramidal. A small tip is convenient for soldering small delicate works or the inside of angles on three-dimensional objects. An iron with changeable tips is very useful. Try different size irons to see how they feel in your hand.

To avoid the nuisance of unplugging the cord when the iron gets too hot, a simple and inexpensive "on-off" line switch should be installed on the cord about 12 to 14 inches from the handle of the iron. If you want to spend extra money, you might invest in a more professional rheostat control unit. A small stand to rest the hot iron on when it is not in use is imperative.

Before a new soldering iron is used, its copper tip must be "tinned." For this procedure, the first step is to clean it by filing the tip to remove all traces of oxidation and soil. Stroke it smoothly in one direction until it is copper pink and shiny, taking care to maintain the original planes of the tip. Brush liquid soldering flux over the tip when it is clean. The flux used for all solder work in this book is liquid oleic (ō-lā-ic) acid. Soldering flux promotes close adhesion between solder and metal; without it the melted solder will roll off the metal in balls. Flux also deters the formation of oxides on the hot surface while solder is applied. Over a period of use, some pitting will accumulate on the iron's tip. Tinning must be repeated from time to time, always starting with a clean filed tip. Solder will not adhere to tarnished or soiled metal. The solder employed both for tinning the copper tip and for joining leads in stained glass work is 60/40 solid-core ⅛-inch wire solder. It contains 60 percent tin and 40 percent lead. The percentage of tin is always placed first in designating solder content. Resin core solders are not suitable for leading stained glass work. They will gum up the glass to the extent that it will be difficult to clean it.

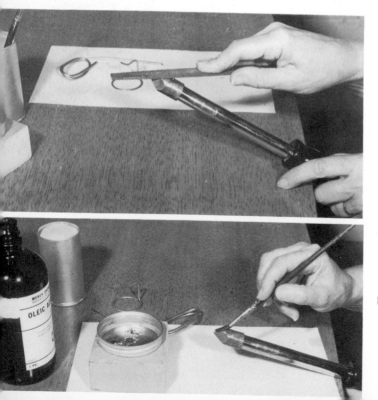

Clean the soldering iron by filing the tip to remove oxidation and soil.

Flux the tip of the iron with oleic acid.

When the iron's tip has been cleaned and fluxed, plug in the iron and heat it. As soon as solder that has been touched to the tip begins to melt, run the solder all over the planes of the tip to cover it with a thin solder coating. If the solder does not adhere to the tip, it may be the iron is too hot. Cool down the tip to the temperature at which it will accept the solder. Keep the tip clean by brushing it with flux occasionally while you are using it. Avoid inhaling the hot flux fumes.

The melting point of the same 60/40 solid core solder used for tinning the iron's tip is just right to use with lead came. The solder melts approximately 10 degrees lower in temperature than lead, which provides an adequate working range. The leads around the juncture area must be cleaned before flux is applied. Scrub the leads carefully at the juncture with a copper wire brush or fine sandpaper. When the joints are shiny, dip the solder wire into oleic acid and dab a few drops on each lead joint with a small brush. To apply solder to the lead, position the tip of the heated iron near the end of the solder wire as it approaches the lead joint and bring them together as they touch the joint. Use the minimum amount of solder, about ⅛ inch, and press it against the joint with the iron's tip riding on top of the bead of solder. Hold it there for a second, then lift it up *before it melts the lead*. It should leave a tiny flat solder puddle. Practice soldering on lead scraps before attempting to solder a cherished project. Fill any gaps between lead joints with little slivers of lead before you attempt to solder them. When you have soldered all the joints between leads, check the junctures one by one to be sure none have been missed; then support the panel carefully with one hand beneath it, turn it over and solder the joints on the reverse side.

The four most common reasons solder does not adhere to lead are: the wrong kind of solder; insufficient or incorrect flux; incorrect soldering iron temperature; and soiled lead.

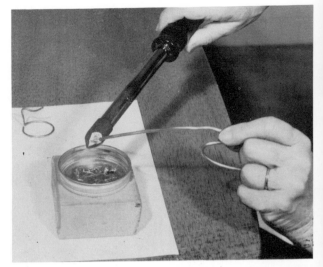

Run the solder over the planes of the working tip on the iron to cover it with a coat of solder. This is called "tinning" the iron.

It is imperative to rest the hot iron on a special small stand when it is not in use. Otherwise you may burn a table or start a fire.

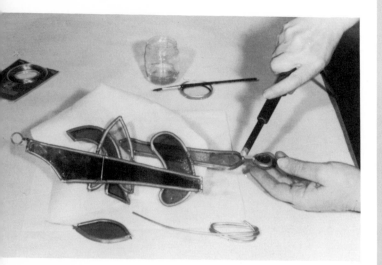

Single glass shapes are leaded as units in a complex construction. The units are soldered together. They are propped on a cushion of folded paper toweling to hold the assemblage in position while the final pieces are soldered to it.

A stained glass suspension. The pieces can be made into a mobile by wiring them separately.

2
Leaded Stained Glass

A BEGINNING

IT IS advisable to make a very simple initial leaded stained glass project before you attempt something more complex. A four-piece colorful stained glass suspension is easy to make, and it requires only a minimum of materials. Creating it will involve many of the techniques you will encounter in fashioning almost any free-form leaded stained glass object. But most important, your own successfully designed and executed stained glass ornament will inspire you to create many other delightful glass objects to beautify your home; and they make wonderful gifts for all ages.

Before you begin, read carefully the introductory sections on cutting glass, applying the lead, and soldering. Make a sketch you like and enlarge it to a full-size drawing divided into three or four sections that are drawn with gently curving or straight lines. Each space will represent a piece of colored glass; each line will represent a strip of lead. Make two carbon

copies of the full-scale drawing, one on firm paper that is cut into small patterns for cutting glass. A second copy is a work drawing on which you will assemble the project. When the glass pieces are cut out, they will be placed on the original drawing nearby to keep them organized and accessible.

Cut out the pattern pieces from the firm paper drawing, using shears to remove a $\frac{1}{16}$-inch paper strip between sections. The narrow space it leaves will represent the place to be occupied by the heart of the lead. With these small paper templates as guides, cut out the glass pieces by following detailed instructions under "Cutting the Glass." To assemble your glass, you will need a three- or four-foot strip of $\frac{1}{4}$-inch rounded H lead, a sharp knife for cutting lead, some blue steel lath nails, and a hammer. In addition, you need a soldering iron, some 60/40 solid core wire solder, and oleic acid for a soldering flux.

Tape the work drawing to a workboard and cut a piece of lead came a little longer than necessary to go completely around the glass

composition. It can be trimmed later. The first glass piece is positioned on its matching space in the work drawing. Its outer edge is inserted into the border lead, which is positioned so it abuts the drawn border line of the design, along its outside. Lath nails are driven into the work-board (right through the paper drawing) close against the outside of the lead; more nails go along the inside bare glass edge to hold the lead and glass securely together while the work proceeds. Cut and fit another lead along one side of the glass with an end trimmed to abut the border lead. Insert the remaining glass pieces into the composition, fitting them one by one with leads that abut the border lead snugly. Lengths of lead fitted between the sides of two glass pieces are always cut about $\frac{1}{16}$ inch shorter at each end than the glass sides, to allow for fitting the remaining bare glass sides into cross-leads. After each glass is inserted, tap it gently into the lead with a small block of wood held between the glass and the hammer. Never strike the bare glass; you may shatter it. As you continue to bend the border lead around the outside of the assemblage, keep it in position with lath nails. Check to assure that they do not press too tightly against the lead and make unsightly dents in it. The nails will all be pulled out when the leads have been soldered.

Once the border lead is in place around the completed composition, trim its two ends for a close fit. Butt them together carefully and anchor them with lath nails. Make certain all pieces are tight and that lead joints fit flush. If you have left any gaps between junctures, fill them with bits of lead that can be soldered over when you apply solder to each joint. When the first side is soldered (follow directions in the "Soldering" section), remove the lath nails, turn the piece over, and solder leads on the reverse side.

To make a hanger for your stained glass composition, double a three- or four-inch length of 18-gauge copper wire, insert the rounded handle of a small brush into the bent loop end and twist it three or four times. Clean and flux the copper wire. Spread the free wire ends apart and solder them to the fluxed leading on top of your hanging. The leaded glass piece can be anchored in a can of sand or vermiculite so both your hands are free to solder. When the oleic acid flux has been cleaned off the glass and lead, your stained glass composition is ready to be hung wherever moving sunlight will infuse it with shimmering beauty.

◀

FLOWERS. Old Dominion Stained Glass Studio. Leaded antique stained glass window. From the Designers' Corner of The Blenko Glass Company, Milton, West Virginia.

Make a full-scale drawing divided into four sections that are drawn with gently curved or straight lines. Trace over it to make two carbon copies, one of which is heavy drawing paper or construction paper.

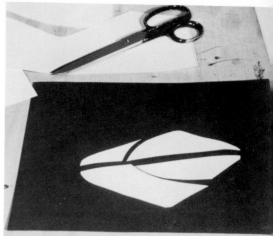

On the heavy paper copy, cut along each side of the inside lines to remove a 1/16'' paper strip between sections. The narrow space remaining represents the place to be occupied by the lead heart.

These four sections of paper are the patterns around which the glass shapes are cut.

The first glass piece is inserted into the border lead. Lath nails temporarily hold the glass and lead in place.

Another lead is cut and fitted along the side of the first glass, and a second glass is inserted. Tap the glass firmly into the lead with a small block of wood.

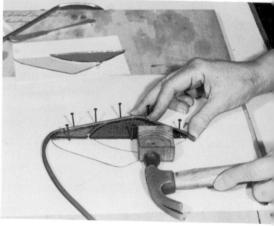

Cut a long lead strip and fit it along the inside edge of the first two glass pieces. To cut the lead, rock the knife gently as you press down. If you press the knife too hard, it will collapse the channels.

Fit lead along a curved edge by holding the glass piece and pressing the lead firmly around the curve.

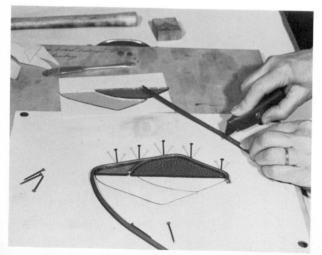

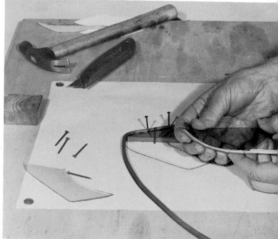

Lengths of lead are always marked and cut a little shorter than the glass edge to allow for insertion of the glass into cross leads. When the location of the cut has been marked, *remove* the lead to cut it. Trim all lead ends so they abut cross-leads snugly parallel.

A small gadget for lifting and working a glass piece securely into the lead is made by bending a short butter knife an inch from the end. Support and brace the assemblage with one hand while the other hand works the knife and glass.

When the last piece is in place, bend the border lead around the completed composition and trim its two ends for a close fit. Hold them in place with lath nails.

Apply flux and solder to each lead joint, then remove the nails and solder the joints on the reverse side.

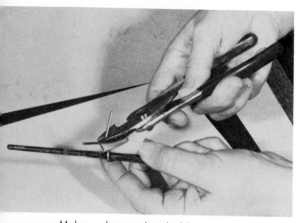

Make a hanger by doubling a 4″ length of copper wire, then twist the loop around a small brush handle.

Clean and flux the wire and lead. Anchor the glass form in a can of sand to hold it so both hands are free to solder the copper wire in position. Pick up some solder with the hot iron tip and run it over the hanger ends while you are pressing them against the lead came. A wooden snap clothespin is convenient for holding the wire hanger in position.

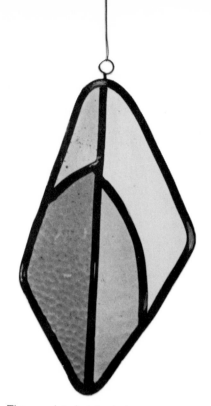

The completed stained glass ornament.

Four units leaded separately and soldered together with open spaces between them.

THE LIGHT TABLE

Although stained glass appears at its best when it is viewed by natural sunlight, this is not always possible in a studio or home workshop situation. As you begin to work with a greater number of stained glass shapes, a good light table can enable you to see relationships of glass colors and their values. It permits you to view colors spread out together. In addition, it is a most important aid for painting on glass. The light table illustrated here is so simple it can be assembled by anyone if the side and end boards and the legs are precut by a lumber company. The table has ball bearing casters installed on the bottom of each leg. These casters with special fixtures for installing them are available at most large hardware stores. When the table is in use, its legs must be anchored in shallow coasters. Casters on the legs are extremely useful when you want to push the light table out of the way. If you prefer a light box instead of a light table, the same specifications can be used by substituting short posts instead of legs. A light box can be set on a table or shelf. Dimensions for the light table are: side walls, 30 by 15 by ¾ inches; end walls, 22½ by 15 by ¾ inches; legs, 30¼ by 1¾ by 1¾ inches.

Nail the side and end boards together to form a box frame. To brace them securely, the legs are held in place in the corners of the box with two large C-clamps while bolts are being installed through holes drilled into the legs as well as the sides and ends of the corners, as shown. The bolts are staggered to prevent interference with one another when they are bolted through the legs to anchor the sides and ends firmly in position. Notice that a space is left at the top of each leg to accommodate ½-inch strips that will be fastened in place with screws ¼ inch below the top edge of the table, to support a sheet of ¼-inch frosted plate glass. Frosted glass is regular plate that can be sandblasted by any large glass company. A heavy plywood bottom for the box or table has corners cut out so it can be slipped over the legs (the table is upended) and fastened in place with screws. The entire interior of the light box part of the table is painted white to give good light reflection and increase illumination under the glass.

Artificial light does not approximate natural daylight for selecting glass, but warm white fluorescent lights help to identify colors and values. Wire the lights together across the bottom of the box. Run the wire through the end wall to a single switch on the outside. A ten-foot cord is a great convenience.

Freestanding stained glass form. Jack Landis.

Freestanding stained glass forms. Jack Landis.

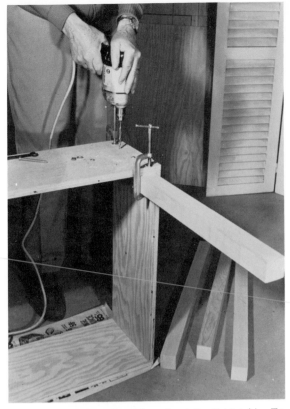

Nail together side and end boards of the light table. To brace them securely, two C-clamps hold them in place while holes are drilled for bolting the legs to the corner.

A space is left at the top of each leg to leave room for wood strips to support the frosted glass top of the table.

A plywood bottom for the light box is slipped over the legs and fastened in place with screws.

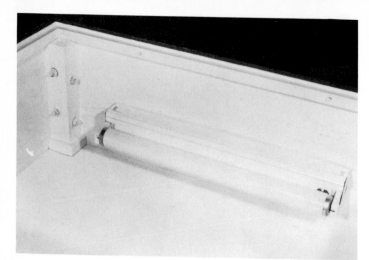

Notice that leg bolts are staggered to allow a leg to be bolted to a side and end board. Lights are installed across the bottom of the box. The interior is painted white.

Illumination shines through to identify colors and values.

CHRYSANTHEMUM. Edward J. Byrne. Three-dimensional glass sculpture. Red, orange, and yellow. 36" diameter.

Edward Byrne works over a stained glass composition on a light table in his Doylestown, Pennsylvania, studio. *Photo by courtesy of* The Philadelphia Inquirer.

PATTERNS AND CARTOONS

A stained glass window or panel begins with a small-scale drawing transposed into a full-size precise pattern or *cartoon*. Two additional copies of the full-size drawing are made: a work drawing and a pattern on heavy paper to be cut into templates. This latter paper must be sturdy but not too thick. Firm drawing paper or smooth heavy wrapping paper will do for these small patterns around which each individual glass piece is cut. Cardboard is too thick; it can prevent the cutting wheel from riding smoothly around each pattern piece.

The cartoon for a leaded stained glass panel must include three important measurements around the border: the full-size line that represents the outer perimeter of the panel's wide border lead; the cut-size line indicating where the glass pieces next to the border will abut the heart of the border lead; and the sight-size line showing the inside edge of the border lead. If you are making a panel or window that must fit into a specified opening, these measurements must be accurate so the outside edge of the perimeter lead will fit exactly.

Because leads may tend to sag, a leaded window that is much higher than three feet tall, should have supportive horizontal one-inch iron T-bars fastened into the window opening at regular intervals to carry the weight of glass and lead. In addition, it requires ½-inch-round horizontal reinforcement bars every foot to brace it against bulging. Five-inch metal ties made of 18-gauge copper wire soldered to the leads of the window can be fastened around the bars. These supports are all designated on the original cartoon. (The making of large stained glass windows is not covered in this book.)

When the full-scale drawing is completed, retrace over the lines of the design with a felt tipped marker to make thick lines that represent the leads of the panel. The heart of each lead forms a thin wall between contiguous glass pieces as they are inserted into the stained glass panel. Space allotted to the lead heart

must be allowed for in cutting out the pattern pieces and their subsequent matching glass shapes.

The next step is to make two copies of the cartoon. First, lay down the firm paper (from which patterns will be cut). On top of it, place a large sheet of good quality carbon paper, carbon side down. If large sheets are not available, lap or butt several small sheets and tape them together on the back with cellophane tape. On top of the carbon paper lay a sheet of paper for the working drawing (to be explained later.) Next comes another large sheet of carbon paper. Finally, the precisely drawn cartoon is positioned on top of all. Thumbtack them all securely to the workboard, pressing each tack firmly through the corners of all these layers to prevent slippage. Some craftsmen prefer to tape each layer to a worktable instead of tacking them to a workboard. When all the layers of paper and carbons are securely in position, take a sharp pencil and trace through the *center* of the thick lines of the design with enough pressure to reach the bottom layer of paper. From time to time as you are tracing, take out one or two thumbtacks to check whether your tracings have gone through all paper layers. Before you take the papers apart, number each space that represents a piece of glass.

When tracing is completed, separate the papers. The *working drawing* will be positioned on the workboard when glazing begins. The *original cartoon* is located nearby so it can be consulted when necessary. Spaces representing pieces of glass are numbered the same on all three drawings. Colors can be written in pencil in case of future changes. The *third heavier drawing* will be cut into small patterns representing the glass pieces. If you have access to a pair of cartoon shears, this is the best tool for cutting out pattern pieces. The shears have a double blade and a single blade; as they cut along the lines of the drawing, a narrow paper strip is removed, leaving a thin space between each pattern to indicate where the heart of the lead goes between glass pieces. Cartoon shears are not always available. A substitute cutting device used by beginners is made by sandwiching a piece of $\frac{1}{16}$-inch cardboard between two single-edged razor blades. They are taped together in two directions. Of course small sharp scissors can be used to cut along each side of the black line to remove it, if you prefer.

To use the razor blade cutting device, position the heavy paper pattern on smooth-topped corrugated cardboard or several sheets of paper to cushion it so the blades of the tool can sink through the pattern and actually cut into it. Draw the blades firmly along so they straddle the pattern lines. Note: the middle, or *cut-size*, line in the *border* of the composition represents the edge of border glass pieces. No narrow paper strip is removed between it and the remaining border area, which is entirely cut away with ordinary scissors. If you use the razor blade tool for cutting out pattern pieces, be sure to use new blades or blades that are sharp. When they are pressed firmly and held perpendicular, both razor blades should cut through the paper. You may find that only one blade seems to be cutting, due to a tendency of most persons to hold the tool on a slant; the other blade will at least leave an indented line that can be cut through with ordinary scissors.

Position each cutout template on the original cartoon over matching numbered spaces. As each template is picked up and a glass shape is cut out around it, both the glass and the template are repositioned on the cartoon. This is the best way to keep all these shapes organized and easily accessible. When all glass pieces for a stained glass composition have been cut, it is time to begin leading them or *glazing* the panel.

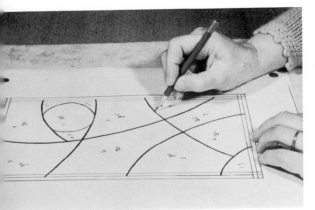

When a design has been drawn full-scale between the three outside lines, trace over the lines of the design with a felt-tipped marker.

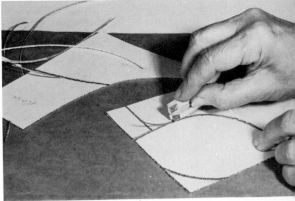

To use the razor-blade cutting device, position the paper pattern on smooth-topped corrugated cardboard, which cushions it so the blades can sink through the pattern and cut it.

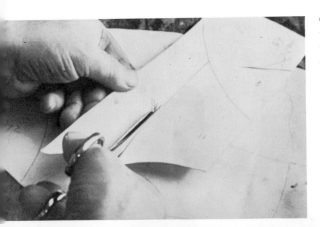

Cutting patterns with a regular pattern shears to allow for lead caming. The single top blade sinks between two lower blades to remove a narrow strip. *Photo by courtesy of Willet Stained Glass Studios.*

LEADING A RECTANGULAR PANEL

When all the glass shapes have been cut for a rectangular panel, tape the work drawing to a workboard that is made of soft wood. Most plywood is too hard to receive the small nails that will hold your work in place temporarily while you are leading it. These nails must be removed from the workboard when leading (glazing) is completed. It is difficult to remove the nails from hard wood without bruising your fingers. Cut two half-inch lath strips, one a little longer than the length of the work drawing and one a little longer than its width. They will guide the placement of the glass and strips of lead. Position them at a right angle to each other on a lower corner of the work drawing with their *inside* edges abutting the *outer full-size* lines of the drawing; this allows room for the flat border leads. Space for these border leads must be included in the original cartoon measurements of the window opening or the frame if you are making a panel. One wood strip runs along the vertical edge of the drawing from top to bottom; the other strip runs along the horizontal lower edge of the work drawing with one of its ends firmly abutting the vertical wooden strip. When both of these strips are nailed into place (with nails going through the paper drawing), it is time to begin leading.

Remember that lead must be stretched and its flanges must be opened before it is used. Stretching it straightens out kinks, firms up the lead, and takes up slack in the soft lead so it fits snugly around the stained glass shapes. If you neglect to stretch it, the lead and glass composition may become wobbly and insecure. When you construct a hanging panel, its hangers should be installed directly above perpendicular lengths of lead in the design; otherwise the border lead to which the small wire hangers are soldered may begin to sag and "let go" the glass after it has hung for a while if the lead is not vigorously stretched before it is used.

To stretch lead, fasten one end of a strip in a strong vise or lead stretcher, grasp the other end of it with pliers and pull firmly until the lead is taut and its channels are straightened. If it is twisted, untwist it between pulls. When you pull on the free end with pliers, hold the lead near the pliers with your other hand and brace yourself with one foot behind you so you do not fall backwards if the lead should break suddenly. Pull firmly until you can feel the lead stretch and become taut. When two persons are working together, each one can pull on an end of the lead until it is stretched. Draw the wet and flattened end of a ¼-inch dowel stick (or glazier's lathekin) along the channels to open them up so different thicknesses of stained glass will fit easily between the flanges. If you are using antique glass, you will find that it has varying thicknesses in one glass sheet, which accounts for its handsome lighter and darker shading of color. When you have stretched a long strip of lead, cut it into shorter convenient lengths and lay it out on a table without doubling or kinking it.

To cut the lead, first score it to mark location of the intended cut; then rock the knife blade gently as you press down cautiously through the lead. Too much or sudden pressure will collapse the channels. It is wise to practice on scraps of lead. The lead-cutting knife used for projects in this book is a standard matt knife with removable blades that can be replaced or sharpened. They are sold in most art supply stores. If you have access to a glazier's curved knife, of course that will be fine; these knives are not always available to the novice.

Place the cartoon beside your workboard with the glass pieces temporarily in place over corresponding drawn spaces. Give it a final check before glazing begins; any changes after this point may waste time and lead. For the border of your panel, cut two stretched and open lengths of ⅜-inch flat H-lead and fit them into the angle of the wooden lath boards you have nailed to the workboard. One lead strip should run along the top of the lower *horizontal lath strip.* The length of the second lead is pressed against the *vertical lath strip* with its bottom end butting down against the horizontal *lead* strip. (Read these instructions again as you follow them in the illustrations on these pages.) Cut the free ends of the leads a little longer than necessary; they will be trimmed when they have been worked into the glass composition. To hold these border leads in place while the first glass pieces are inserted, you may tack the free ends to the workboard temporarily. Make sure the two lengths of lead are butted firmly together in the lower corner. Some craftsmen prefer to pinch the lower end of the vertical lead and slip it into the horizontal lead instead of butting them. Either way, avoid leaving gaps between lead joints that will create problems when you are soldering them.

When the two border leads are securely in place, check their flanges to see whether they are still open along their lengths. If they are not, they can be opened with a handy gadget called a "stopping knife," which you can make by bending a short butter knife about an inch from the end. Or a slender steel table knife can be shortened, ground smooth, and bent near the end. When you have cleared the lead channels, press the first glass piece into the channels where they meet at the corner. Here again, the stopping knife is useful. Slip it under the glass to lift and work it deeper into the corner channels.

The next important step is to place a small block of wood against the glass piece and tap it firmly but gently into the leads. This procedure must be followed after every piece or two are placed, if you would have a snugly fitting firm leaded glass composition. Fit a lead piece into place along each side of the corner glass piece, butting one end of the lead against the border lead. When you have evaluated how much to cut that end of lead so it will abut at an angle parallel to the border lead for a snug fit, remove it and trim it. Trim the other lead end just a little shorter than the glass to allow for insertion of the glass into the cross-lead that divides it from the next row of glass shapes. Build up pieces of glass contiguous to the first corner glass, fanning out from it and supporting it. As each piece of glass is fitted with lead and inserted into bordering leads, tap it gently with the wood block.

As you are building up the glass design, check the drawing under your work to be sure each piece coincides with drawn lines. Sometimes a piece may need a minor amount of grozing (chipping) before it will fit into its designated space. But first tap it in firmly to be sure it is seated and really needs grozing; pieces that are cut accurately and tapped into the leads securely should need very little or no trimming. When you are inserting the glass, avoid surrounding an empty space to the point that the next glass piece cannot be slid into it without requiring the removal of some of the glass already in position.

After each glass is fitted with lead and seated, secure it in place *temporarily* with thin sharp blue steel lath nails driven close beside the lead and bare glass sides, two or three nails to the piece. Take care not to press the nails into the lead or you may have a ragged-looking lead when the nails are removed. The nails are pulled out along the working side of each piece as adjoining leads and glass are positioned. The traditional and useful leading nails (or horseshoe nails) used by professional craftsmen are not easy for the novice to locate. They are nonexistent in some localities. Steel lath nails will serve our purpose very well for simple projects.

Once the glass and leads are all in place, it is time to fit the last two border leads into position. Inspect each glass edge and lead end where they abut the border. If any glass protrudes over the middle line (cut-size line) of the border, it should be tapped in firmly with the wooden block to determine whether looseness in the assemblage caused the bulge. If there is still some glass extending over the line, remove the piece and groze it to fit, or better yet, replace it with a new piece redesigned to fit. Trim the lead ends to make a smooth border juncture. Finally, the wide flat border leads are positioned over the glass and smaller lead ends; two more lath strips are nailed into position against them to hold them in place. When you have inspected your work and filled any lead joint gaps with bits of lead, it is time to solder the work. Do not remove the nails from the lath strips until the first side of the panel is completely soldered. (Read carefully the instructions detailed in the section "Soldering.") Then remove the nails, support the panel with one hand braced under it, and when you have turned it over carefully solder the second side.

When both sides of the panel have been soldered, push gray glazing compound (putty) against the leads with your thumb and work it under them wherever possible. It holds the glass tight and makes a window weatherproof. Clean up excess putty by running a pointed stick along the leads. The flat border leads are pressed firmly with a putty knife to work out excess glazing compound. To absorb and remove the remainder of putty and the oleic acid, sprinkle a couple of handfuls of whiting (calcium carbonate) over the panel and scrub it around with a stiff brush. Brush away the dust and dirt with a soft brush and rags. The glass is cleaned in the usual way with detergent water or regular glass cleaner.

Two ½" lath strips guide the placement of the glass and lead. Nail them at right angles to one another on a lower corner of the work drawing. The glass pieces are laid out in correct sequence on the paper patterns beside the work.

Fit two lengths of lead into the angle of the wood lath boards. The first glass pieces will be inserted into the corner of the leads.

Press the first glass piece into the lead channels where they meet at the corner.

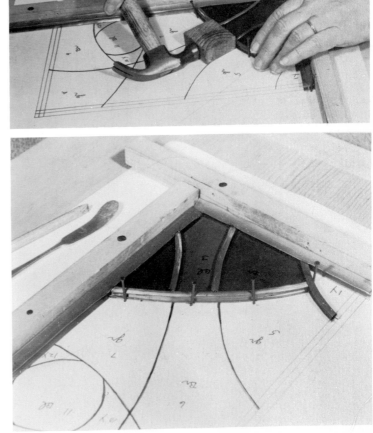

A short bent knife (stopping knife) lifts up the glass to help seat it into the channels of the leads.

Place a small wood block against the leaded glass and tap it firmly to make a snug-fitting composition.

Small lath nails hold the composition in place temporarily. The leads and glass follow lines in the drawing.

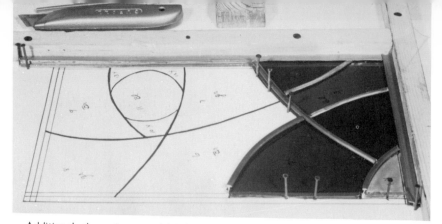

Additional glass pieces and leads are inserted. The bare glass edge borders the middle cut-size line.

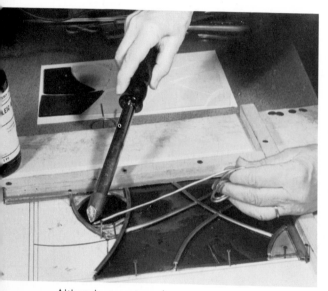

Although a rectangular or square panel is usually leaded up completely before it is soldered, a small grouping of pieces in a larger composition is sometimes soldered into place to hold it secure as the panel is assembled.

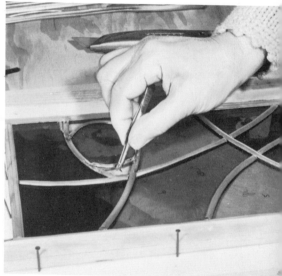

All glass and leads are in place; the final border leads are positioned and anchored with nails and a third lath strip. Fill any gaps in lead junctures with bits of lead.

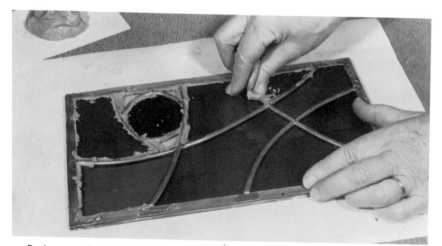

Push gray glazing compound (putty) against and under each lead with your thumb. It holds the glass tight and will make a window panel weatherproof.

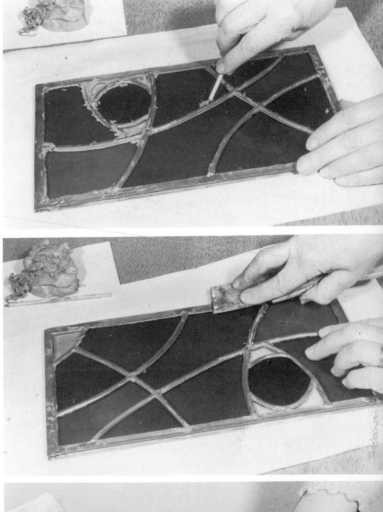

Remove excess putty by running a pointed dowel stick, meat skewer, or pencil along all the leads.

Flat border leads are pressed smooth with a putty knife to work out excess compound.

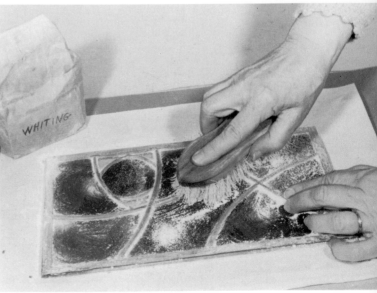

Clean away scraps of glazing compound and oleic acid by sprinkling several handfuls of whiting (calcium carbonate) over the panel; scrub it diligently with a stiff brush. Clean away remaining crumbs of whiting and putty with a soft brush and rags. Then clean the glass with regular glass cleaner. The panel can be hung, or you can make three additional panels to combine into a lantern as shown on the following pages.

A FOUR-PANEL LANTERN

The panels for a four-sided lantern are individually formed before they are assembled. Follow the instructions given in the preceding section. Designs may be similar for all four panels, or they may alternate. They can, of course, be different in all four panels, but this would be a more complex undertaking. It is advisable to keep them simple and to employ medium and light colors. The electric bulbs used in stained glass lanterns do not transmit the kind of illumination that comes from a sunny sky. Dark glass transmits very little light.

To shield the light fixture from sight, the lantern top can be formed of metal or opalescent glass. A top made from glass sections is not the easiest kind for an initial project. The top for the demonstration lantern is an upside-down copper tray, the kind sold in metal enameling supply shops. You will be delighted to find a variety of copper trays in many sizes and shapes: square, round, octagonal, and others. A ⅜-inch hole must be cut in the metal top to accommodate electric wiring and a top ring for holding the chain or rope hanger. If you cannot cut the hole, any metalwork shop will do it for a nominal fee.

Panel dimensions for the demonstration lantern are 6½ by 11 inches. Border leads are ⅜-inch flat H-leads; leads for the panel design are ¼ inch, with the exception of the rounded glass piece, which is fitted with 3/16-inch lead. The copper tray top is 7½ inches square. On each panel side edge, the border lead flange, which faces toward the *inside* of the lantern, is bent to about a 90-degree angle to the panel, permitting the *outside* flanges at each corner to butt together. Stand the first two panels on end at a right angle to one another, as illustrated in the accompanying photograph. Prop them in position with any straightedged blocks such as bricks. Pinch the bent lead flanges together down the inside of the corner and solder them along the edge. A small soldering iron tip is very convenient for inside corners.

Set the third panel in position and support it with additional bricks. Once it is soldered in place, lay the assemblage down with the remaining open side toward the table top. Brace the two panels that rest on the table with bricks laid against their outside surfaces while the fourth panel is positioned between them and soldered, first from one end, then from the other end. At this point, the lantern is set upside down so 8-gauge copper wire that has been annealed can be soldered into the bottom lead channels and around corners to brace them. The wire is annealed by heating it red hot, then dousing it in water. Annealing metal makes it pliable and easy to work. If it stiffens as you work it, anneal it again. Until the square top is soldered to the lantern, care must be exercised in handling the work to keep the four joined panels in a right-angled position. Once the firm metal top is soldered in place, it will keep the lantern squared.

If you want to conceal the outside juncture crack between the leads that run down the length of each outside corner of the lantern, split some ⅜-inch or ½-inch flat H-leads down through the heart with a chisel or shears to make flat lead strips. Tack a strip to each corner with solder, top and bottom. Press the soft lead smoothly against and around each corner with your fingers and solder it in several additional places along the edges. Set the completed body of the lantern aside while the square copper top (with a ⅜-inch hole cut in it) is scrubbed clean with scouring powder, rinsed, dried, and set upside down on a bench wheel.

The solder used for bonding the copper top to the lantern is 40/60 low fusing self-fluxing paste solder called "Fast." This type solder is doubtless available under other trade names. Copper oxidizes so quickly when heat is applied that the 60/40 solid core wire solder used for leading cannot be used for soldering copper to lead. An exception is when copper wire (which heats up rapidly) is soldered to make hangers for suspending stained glass mobiles. Self-fluxing paste solder excludes air from the metal surface, which deters oxidation and allows bonding readily. Set the lantern upside down on the copper top and mark its intended location with a pencil. Then remove the lantern and brush paste solder along each section of the inverted top (copper tray) over the pencil marking.

Set the lantern upside down again on the metal top, carefully matching the lantern to the brushed solder. There are bound to be a few crevices between the lantern and the metal top. Cut some small flat slivers of lead and brush solder on both surfaces of the little lead pieces. For extra reinforcement, insert two or three of them securely against the juncture between the lantern and the metal top on each side. Once all the small lead bits are in place, it is time to apply the heat. Low heat is sufficient to melt this solder; a propane cylinder torch, the kind bought in hardware stores, will work very well. Hold a length of asbestos paper in front of the stained glass and leads of the lantern to protect them while you apply gentle heat from below the copper as illustrated. Hold the flame under the area to be soldered and *play it back and forth slowly*. The tip of the flame should be held about an inch from the metal. Keep close watch over it. As soon as the solder turns silver and shiny, *remove the torch*. Leave the lantern undisturbed for several minutes before you set it upright so the solder can harden.

Most electric lamp and fixture stores carry an assortment of accessories for lanterns. The parts used for the four-panel lantern shown here are a lamp ring (also called a *loop*), a threaded *nipple*, a *light socket*, and a *separator plate* that fits between the metal lantern top and the threaded nipple. Decorative chain is used to hang the lamp or lantern.

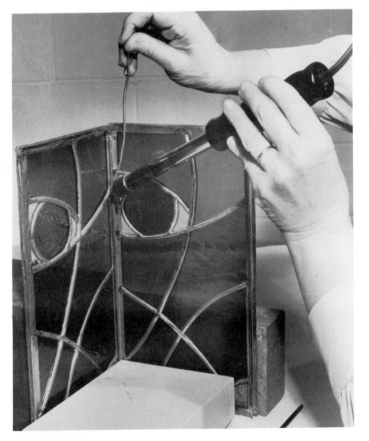

Stand the first two panels on end at a right angle. Prop them securely in place with any straight-edged blocks such as bricks. Solder them along the inside of the corner angle.

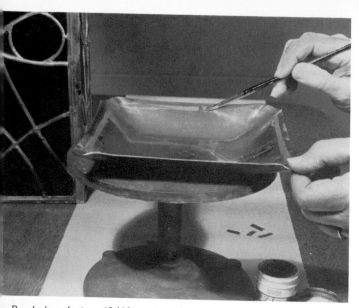

Brush low fusing 40/60 paste solder along each section of the copper top where the lantern will be positioned. Notice the small lead pieces that will be soldered into the juncture between the lantern and its top.

Hold asbestos in front of the glass and lead to protect them from the torch as you play it slowly along under the solder.

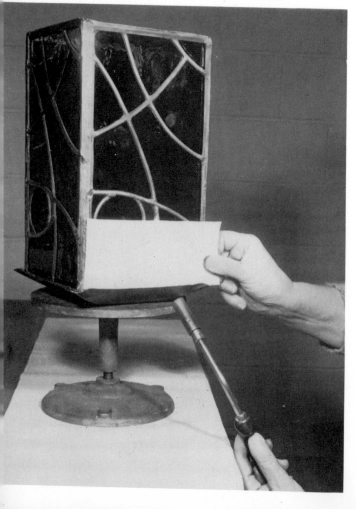

The completed lantern with electric fittings. Antique stained glass provides shimmering color.

Electrified lantern. Bette Warner. 20'' tall, 10'' diameter. Antique stained glass.

Lead camed stained glass window. Designed by Jack Landis and Kathy Clark. Executed by Jack Landis. Center is a purple rondel; the background is clear ripple glass; the main pattern is mixed purple and white opalescent with dark areas in red cathedral glass; border is mixed green opalescent. The window was made for a restored home of the Federal Period in the historic Oregon district of Dayton, Ohio, owned by Shirley and Jack Landis. *Photo by Kathy Clark.*

A FREE-FORM STAINED GLASS PANEL

There are two chief differences between leading the free-form shape and leading a rectangular or square panel. First, the leads in the free-form design sometimes extend outward and become part of the border; there is no continuous framing lead. For this reason, ¼-inch H-lead is used throughout the illustrated free-form composition. The second chief difference, lead junctures are soldered as your work progresses. Instead of leading from a corner and working out in a fan-shape direction, apply and solder the leads straight across the panel composition, beginning at any point on the panel perimeter. In the demonstrated design, the center glass piece, number 8, is leaded as part of the first row of work. Otherwise the space for it would be encircled by the border pieces; the center glass could not be worked into its designated position. Be sure to tap the glass into the lead with a wood block as you work. If a glass piece does not fit correctly, replace it. One glass shape bulging over encircling lines will prevent contiguous pieces from fitting into their indicated positions.

The small leaf shapes along the outer edge of the design have well-defined corners. To keep this crisp effect, the lead is cut at each corner and the ends are mitered together in a point. Cut the lead ends so the juncture appears to continue on a line with the point of the glass corner.

When each glass piece has been tapped into place with the wood block, anchor it with lath nails along the working edge while you solder the lead joint. Then remove the nails between pieces and fit another glass with lead and so on. Do not remove any nails from around the outside edge of the panel until the soldering is completed. These border nails hold the panel firmly in place while you work on it. When soldering is completed, support the panel underneath with one hand, carefully turn it over and solder the reverse side. Glazing a leaded stained glass hanging panel is optional, but many persons do glaze hangings to give them a firmness and finished quality. To complete the project, solder a wire hanger to the top as described in the section, "A Beginning."

Glass shapes are laid out on the light table to check colors and values.

The interior leads in this free-form design extend outward to become part of the border glass lead, then they curve into the interior again. There is no continuous framing lead.

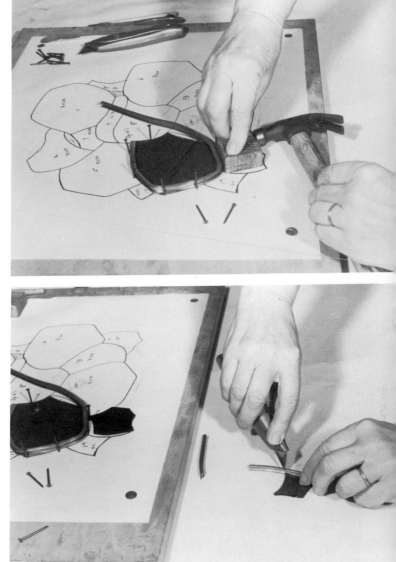

Small leaf shapes have well-defined corners. The lead is cut apart at each corner and ends are mitered together again.

Lead joints in a free-form design are soldered as the leading progresses.

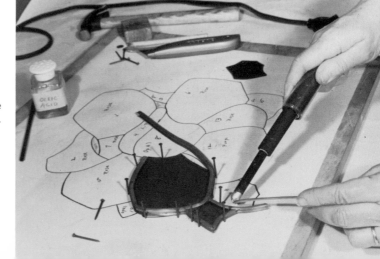

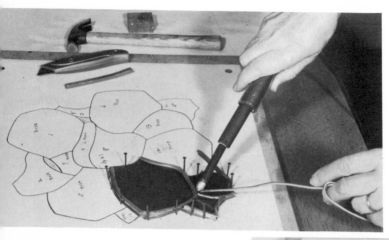

Apply and solder the leads straight across the panel. Include the center glass piece with the first row.

As you work, anchor the leads all around the edge of the assemblage with lath nails until the project is complete, then remove the nails.

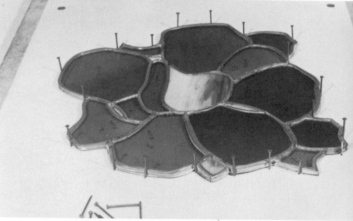

A colorful antique glass panel makes a decorative and striking window treatment against the sun or snow. Colors are opalescent rose and green for the center and one leaf. Rose, amethyst, olive, and green for the rest of the flower.

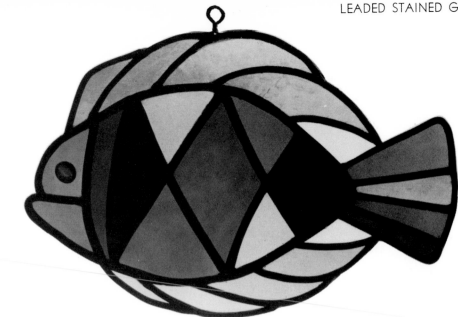

Lead camed antique glass fish. Bright blue, green, and red. The body is leaded first, then the tail and fins beginning with the rear fins. Open spaces are left between the rear fins and body.

COMBINING STAINED GLASS TECHNIQUES

Colored glass is an exciting medium for craftsmen. Although a form may be simple, the moment sunlight floods through it, brilliant shimmering color delights the eye. Pieces of contrasting bonded stained glass and crushed glass sparkle and glow. You can provide a subtle layered effect with small shapes fused to glass that will be bonded, leaded, or bent. Add an exotic touch to dull leads by rubbing metallic paste finishes over them to transform them with rich coloring. For an exciting way to create with glass, make use of a variety of materials and methods to add color and texture wherever you want them.

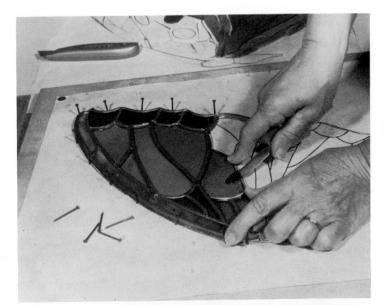

A LARGE BUTTERFLY HANGING

Leading for a large stained glass butterfly begins at the border of the top right wing and progresses down the panel.

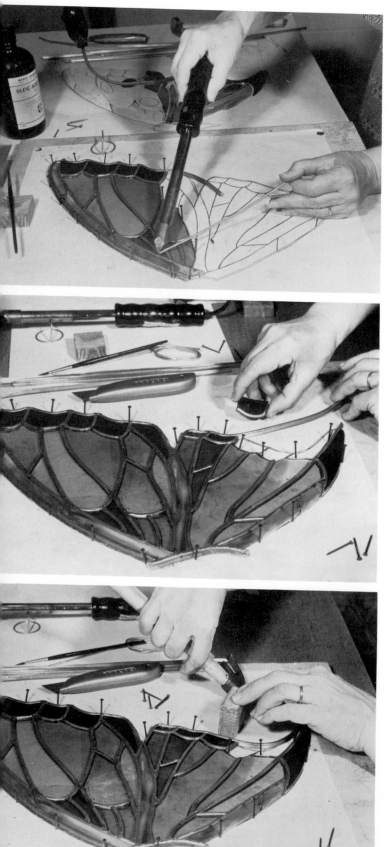

Leading along each side of the wing sections is continuous; it is soldered together at each wing tip. After every two or three glass pieces are inserted, they are tapped securely into the lead and soldered.

One piece of lead is bent around two sides of each border scalloped piece before it is inserted into the border leading.

Tap each piece firmly so it lines up with the drawn design underneath it.

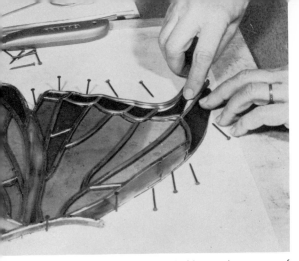

Final wing pieces are inserted. Notice that some of the nails are removed so border leads can be fitted.

The last lead is fitted along a wing edge. Glass shapes are worked into the leading with the small knife. An end of lead is left extending one-half inch long at wing tip and is curved to give a decorative effect and to provide a hanging hook at each upper wing tip.

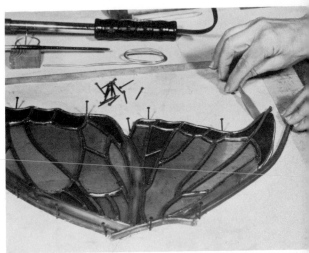

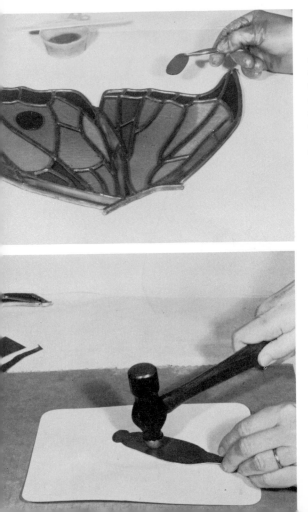

After the glass has been thoroughly cleaned, wing spots are epoxied into position. The epoxy is dried completely. Finally, the wing is turned over and soldered at each joint. The leads are puttied to give added firmness to the composition. Scrub away the soil and putty with whiting as described earlier. A second wing is prepared in reverse, identical to the first.

A hammered, contoured copper body is made in two sections. Brush 40/60 low-fusing paste solder along the edges of each half, inside and outside. Bind them securely with regular jeweler's binding wire around the head and tail and insert the body into the leading of the wings where they normally join the body.

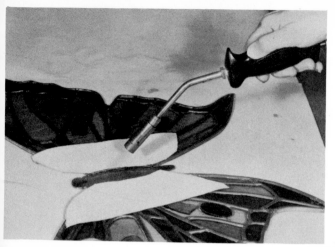

Two pieces of asbestos paper protect the glass and lead while a propane torch applies the low heat required to melt this solder.

Achieve a final rich effect on any of your leaded stained glass creations by rubbing the leads and solder with any of the nontoxic lustrous metallic paste finishes. They come in dozens of beautiful metallic colors. The butterfly leading is covered with bronze wax paste. The antennae are made from a doubled wire soldered to the head with 40/60 solder.

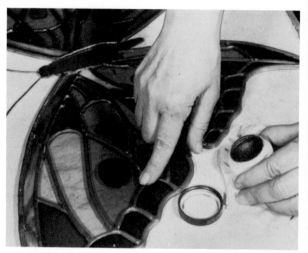

The completed butterfly is 26" from wing tip to wing tip. It is 16" deep. It can be made strong by soldering slender steel rods on the back side that cross the body diagonally behind the opalescent edges of the wings. This butterfly is adequately supported with very fine steel wires that suspend it from the small lead "hooks" at the tips of the upper wings. It is deep blue, green, orange, and lavender, and a very light blue glass over most of the butterfly gives it a gossamer fragile appearance, even though it is such a large composition.

SMALL WINDOW PANELS

Glass for a small leaded window panel is spread out on the light table for a final check of color relationships. The separate glass piece that has been removed from the composition will be painted and fired before it is leaded into place.

The glass piece is taped to a design over the light table so it can be revolved as painting progresses. A wood bridge is not needed for this one glass piece.

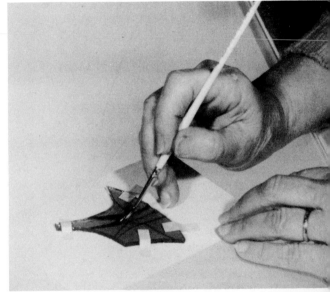

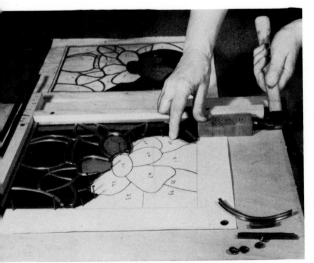

A complex design with irregularly shaped pieces must be braced securely with one hand while they are tapped firmly into position in leading. Otherwise they will slide out of place when they are tapped with the wood block. Geometric compositions are easier to control. Glass pieces must coincide with the drawn design beneath them.

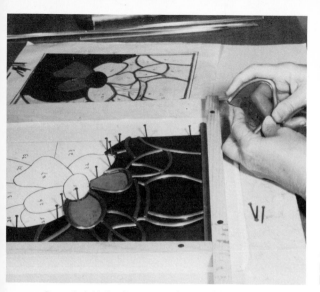

Rounded H lead is pressed smoothly all around the curved piece before it is inserted into the assemblage.

When the panel is completely leaded and soldered on both sides, the glass is cleaned thoroughly to remove oil from the oleic acid. Several small glass shapes are epoxied into place for a sparkling effect. It is wise to wear gloves when you use epoxy products. Avoid inhaling the fumes.

The panel gleams with color against the sunlit snow. It is puttied into place against the regular window glass.

3
Bonded Glass

INTRODUCTION TO BONDING

A BONDED glass panel begins with a sheet of colorless double-strength window glass or plate glass for a base. When it has been cleaned carefully, small stained glass shapes in various sizes, thicknesses, and colors are epoxied to it. Because the bonded glass composition does not have the supportive dark linear design quality of leaded glass, some definite variation in value must be provided with dark glass accents or dark grouting worked between the applied glass shapes. When you become bolder, you may add small chips of faceted glass, segments of clear glass adhered flat or on their edges, and even materials other than glass. Although your first efforts may produce a few cracked and shivered glass assemblages, you should be rewarded eventually with exciting and delightful ideas for design. Improved technical mastery will soon translate them into successful glass art.

The undulating quality that gives beauty to antique glass makes it difficult to bond without creating some irregular bubbles be-tween it and the clear glass base, an effect that can be quite decorative. However, if you do not care for this effect, it is suggested that you use rolled cathedral glass, which has one smooth surface suitable for bubble-free bonding. The glass must be prepared *before the epoxy is mixed*. For safety's sake, all glass edges are sanded smooth under water. Wash stained glass and clear glass base with hot detergent water, rinse it in warm water, and dry it completely. Take care to support the glass by its edges to avoid transferring skin oil to the clean surfaces. Epoxy will not bond securely to damp or soiled glass.

Epoxy adhesives come in two containers: one is the resin and the other is the hardener. The two components must be blended thoroughly before use. For very small projects, epoxy can be bought in tubes. Epoxy is bought in quarts or gallons for large important projects. Be sure to use *epoxy* resin and hardener especially formulated for glass on glass bonding.* *Polyester* resins usually shrink when

* Epoxy used for *sheet glass* bonding projects in this book is Thermoset Resin #600 with Thermoset Hardener #37.

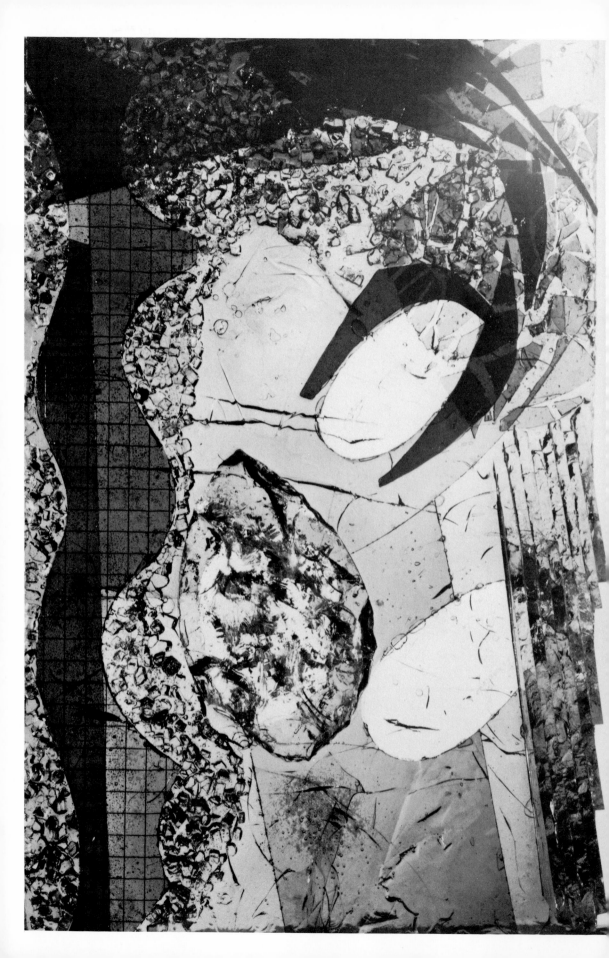

they dry and they may set up stresses in the glass that can cause large bonded glass projects to crack.

Before epoxying begins, clear the table top and the surrounding area where the work will be done. The table *must be level.* Otherwise pieces may slide out of position while the adhesive is drying. Mix only the amount you can apply in 30 to 40 minutes. Work diligently so all pieces are epoxied and pressed into place before the adhesive starts to set. The resin, the hardener, the pieces of glass, and the working room temperature should all be kept between 75° and 85°F throughout the process. Make certain the area is well ventilated and avoid inhaling the fumes. It is advisable to wear thin plastic gloves that can be bought in hardware or paint stores, when you work with epoxy resins; some skins are sensitive to resin.

A thin film of the epoxy cement provides the greatest adhesive strength. Epoxy has a different coefficient of expansion from glass. When stained glass is bonded to plate glass or double-strength window glass in large windows or panels, stresses are set up in the glass if it is exposed to bright sunlight for long periods of time. A large stained glass panel will absorb heat faster than clear colorless glass and it will tend to expand; the darker the color of the glass, the greater is the strain. If large sheets of stained glass, or even large segments, are encased entirely in resin top and bottom, they are almost certain to crack when the stained glass begins to expand. But a thin layer of the adhesive applied beneath stained glass pieces causes less strain and less hazard of breaking when the pieces are no longer than eight inches. If a design calls for a long piece of dark glass, use a series of shorter pieces spaced $\frac{1}{16}$ inch between segments. Follow the epoxy manufacturer's instructions. Remember, *other resins may mix differently.* Do not mix up more epoxy than you can apply in 30 to 40 minutes. A half ounce of resin and a half ounce of hardener make a considerable amount. The beginner tends to mix too great a quantity at one time.

Once the epoxy ingredients have been blended the required amount of time, pick up a clean piece of glass, spread it evenly and thinly with epoxy, position it exactly and press it firmly in place on the clear sheet of glass, following the drawn design underneath the window glass. Continue epoxying and applying glass pieces and pressing firmly. If you plan to apply grout between the glass shapes when the epoxy has dried, the resin that oozes out between glass pieces when you press them down must be removed with a toothpick or other means and wiped on paper toweling. If the epoxy is left to fill the cracks, there will be no place for the grout. By this time you may have smeared some epoxy on the pieces of stained glass. Do not be too concerned; as soon as the epoxy has started to set and become rubbery, but before it hardens, it can be scraped away with a single-edged razor blade and removed completely with epoxy solvent. Moisten the cloth lightly so solvent does not run under the epoxied glass and ruin the epoxy's adhesive qualities. Always wear plastic gloves when you use any kind of solvent; if this is neglected, the solvent may carry chemicals deep into your skin. And of course do not clean your hands with solvents.

◄

Bonded stained glass exhibition panel. Willet Stained Glass Studios. Farbigem process.

BONDING GLASS—RANDOM SHAPES

Shaped glass remnants obtained from a glass studio or an art glass supply company often make interesting and beautiful compositions when they are bonded to window glass with epoxy resin. Studio glass scraps separated from actual glass designs have exciting and useful shapes. For a first project, it is advisable to select light colorful hues until you are experienced in using darker glass for accents in a composition.

Lay a sheet of double-strength window glass on the light box or on white paper so the glass colors are easily seen. Spread a number of glass pieces directly on the glass sheet; move them around until you have a pleasing arrangement. They may be laid closely together or with spaces between them. Some of them may require minor trimming with short straight cuts or grozing. (See "Cutting the Glass.") When you have made a final selection of glass shapes, wash, rinse, and dry them as explained earlier. The clean colored glass pieces are positioned on clean paper to one side of the window glass in the same order they will have when they are bonded to the clear glass. It is helpful to make a full-size drawing of the final arrangement of the pieces, and to put it under the window glass to guide placement of the epoxied stained glass.

Read carefully all the directions on epoxy containers before you mix the resin and hardener as specified. The two parts must be blended thoroughly. As soon as you apply the adhesive in a thin coat to the underside of a glass shape, press it firmly into position on the clear glass pane. If you use a spreading stick, it can be wiped clean with a rag or paper towel that you can discard at little cost. Should you apply epoxy with a brush, in a short time your brush may accumulate a mass of resin in various stages of hardening and it may have to be discarded. When all the glass is in place, let the panel dry for at least 24 hours. If any pieces are moved after the epoxy starts to set, the epoxy will show up as cloudy distortions in the glass. When the adhesive has set, grout may be applied between the glass.

Mix powdered grout with water to damp clay consistency. Pack it between glass pieces with a tiny spatula or cardboard edge, then smooth it evenly. Remove all surplus grout from the tops of glass pieces immediately; it will be very difficult to remove after it sets. *To keep grout from cracking* while it dries, cover the panel closely with plastic sheeting for eight hours. White grout in small projects can be painted with India ink when it is dry. Grouting for projects in this book is ceramic tile grout bought in commercial tile stores. Companies that make this grout also sell a coloring material to blend with the dry powder before it is mixed with water.

Spread random stained glass pieces directly on the clear glass sheet and move them around until you have a pleasing arrangement.

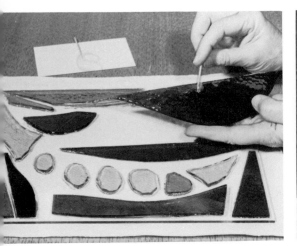

Apply epoxy in a thin even coat to the underside of each glass piece and press it firmly into place.

As soon as grout is packed into all spaces between the glass, remove all excess grout with water and a sponge before the grout dries. It is difficult to remove after it has set.

The grout can be painted with coats of India ink. Grout is also mixed with grout color before it is used.

Black grout and glass make contrasting patterns.

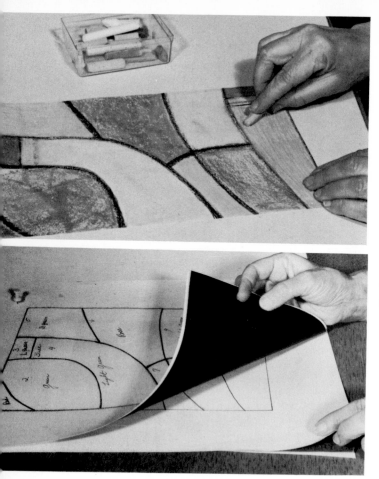

A design is drawn full-scale in color for a small bonded panel.

Three identical drawings are made of the panel design.

BONDING GLASS—CUT SHAPES

Three identical drawings are made for a project in bonded glass that is designed and cut to a definite pattern. Unlike a leaded glass project, only one border line is made on each copy. This line indicates the outer limits of applied stained glass shapes. One drawing, on firm paper, is cut into small templates representing glass pieces that will be applied to the clear glass base. The glass shapes are cut out around the small patterns, carefully washed and dried, and arranged in their correct sequence on the cartoon. The work drawing is taped to the workboard. A sheet of clean double-strength window glass is positioned on top of it so extra drawing paper extends beyond the clear glass. The window glass base must be the size of the drawn design *plus a margin of at least ¼ inch* all around the edge

to allow clear space for mounting the finished panel. Tape the glass sheet securely to the drawing so the masking tape extends over this ¼-inch margin all around the glass edge; no stained glass or epoxy is applied to this margin. Putty or thin wood strips can cover the edge when the completed panel is installed or framed. The masking tape must be removed when the epoxy begins to set and become rubbery, but *before it hardens*. Otherwise the epoxy will seal it firmly to the glass.

A heavy cardboard or plastic container, plastic measuring spoons, two plastic ¼-cup measures, a small scale such as a postage scale, stirring sticks, spreaders, and a can of epoxy solvent that should be bought at the same time the resin is purchased are placed on a nearby shelf. If the instructions on the resin container specify equal amounts of resin and hardener by volume rather than by weight, the scales are

One drawing is cut into small patterns. Glass shapes are cut out around the small patterns, one side at a time.

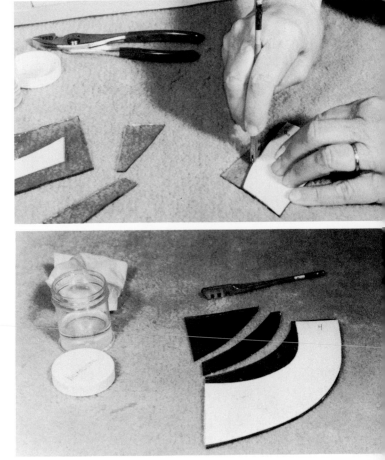

Deep curves are cut in shallow sections, one at a time.

not necessary. For large projects, the scale would be proportionately larger if it is required. When the entire amount of resin and hardener in the containers is mixed at one time, no scale is necessary. But remember, when the two components are blended, they must be used up in the brief length of time specified on the containers. Clean rags or paper toweling are needed to clean up after the epoxying is completed.

When everything is ready, don your plastic gloves and prepare to mix the epoxy. The success of your bonded project will depend on *following exactly* the manufacturer's instructions, so read them again. Mixing directions will vary for different resin-hardener combinations. Thermoset Resin #600 and Thermoset Hardener #37 were used for these bonding projects. This resin becomes cloudy when it is first mixed with hardener due to tiny bubbles

formed through chemical action. The two components are mixed very thoroughly. About twenty minutes after they have been mixed, the cloudiness begins to disperse and then the epoxy is applied. As it dries it becomes quite clear and colorless, unless it has been applied too thick.

Check the epoxied stained glass pieces from time to time to make certain they have not shifted. As long as they move quite easily, they can be slid gently back into place. If some pieces touch one another at certain points and are farther apart at others, it adds a pleasing casual effect, typical of bonded glass work. Do not move the glass shapes once the epoxy begins to set. When all the glass pieces are pressed into place, leave the panel undisturbed (except for cleaning up) for a minimum of 24 hours. The bonding achieves its greatest strength after seven days.

The narrow piece of glass is separated with pliers while one hand bends the larger section outward.

Each cut piece of glass is positioned on the cartoon along with its pattern piece, to keep all these small shapes organized and convenient.

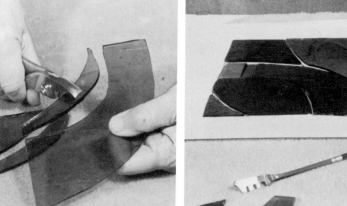

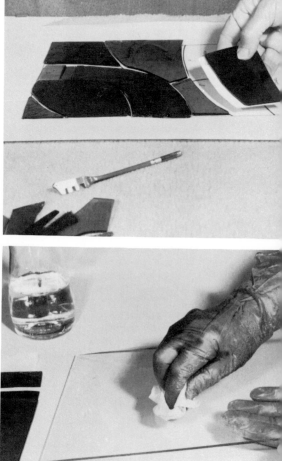

Sand the edges of newly cut glass to remove thin sharp slivers that appear along new cuts.

The glass is cleaned and dried. It is wise to wear gloves whenever you work with chemicals.

Tape the work drawing to the work-board. Tape the glass sheet securely to the drawing with masking tape extending over a ¼″ margin all around the glass edge.

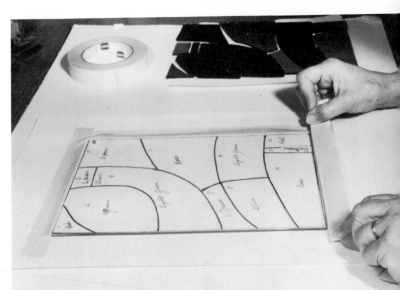

Spread epoxy thin and even over each glass shape and press it firmly in place on the clear glass sheet following the drawn design under the glass.

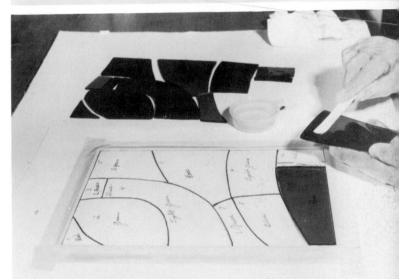

Dry black grout colorant is mixed with white grout before water is added. The colored grout will be lighter when dry.

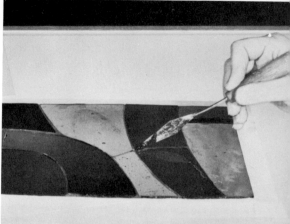

Mix the grout, the colorant, and enough water to make a paste consistency. Blend it with a small spatula. Clean off the surplus grout before it dries.

Work the grout into each crevice until it is even with the glass surface. Then press it smoothly with a spatula. Clean off the surplus grout before it dries.

Textured antique glass panels are decorative and cheery in any window.

BONDED GLASS MOSAICS

Few glass methods are simpler yet more effective than making a colorful glass mosaic. This ancient art form fits easily into today's life style, providing aesthetic beauty and often structural reinforcement to a surface that may be as great as a wall or as diminutive as an ear ring. Glass, unlike other mosaic materials, is often transparent, although it may be translucent or opaque as well. The glass is cut into small shapes called tesserae (pronounced tesseri̅). The professional mosaic artist may skillfully mix unusual shapes and materials. By far the most mosaics are made with fairly uniform, more or less rectangular shaped tesserae that are from ½ to 1 inch long, usually laid side by side in rows to form a design. Glass is seldom mixed with other mosaic materials. Because glass is usually transparent or translucent, its true beauty is realized when the base or backing for the mosaic is either transparent, as sheet glass or plastic, or if it is opaque it must be finished in a very light reflective neutral color or white. Plywood, masonite, glass, and plastic are materials commonly used for the base or backing of a glass mosaic.

The base for the illustrated project is the top of a previously discarded small table. It is completely refinished and prepared before the mosaic is begun. Old varnish is stripped from the entire table. The top is sanded, then given a coat of light cream-colored house paint. After it has dried, it is sanded lightly for better bondage with the adhesive that will hold the glass tesserae in place. The rest of the table is sanded smooth, then given a coat of cherry wood-stain, topped with clear shellac and rubbed with paste wax. Care must be taken to keep wax and oil off the surface where the mosaic will be applied to ensure that the adhesive will hold the tesserae firmly attached. Regular household glue will not work for this project. It adheres to wood and other porous materials but not to glass which is too smooth, hard, and nonporous. An excellent glass adhesive is two-component epoxy resin made especially for bonding glass as discussed in the section "Bonded Glass." Narrow spaces are left between the tesserae for grouting.

Grout is a very fine durable mortar used in all kinds of mosaics. To bond a grouted glass mosaic, epoxy the glass pieces individually to the base, leaving narrow spaces for the grout between the tesserae. When the adhesive is quite dry, the grout mixture is worked into the cracks with a rubber spatula. Regular bathroom and kitchen tile grout is excellent for glass mosaics, and it is water-resistant.

Begin the mosaic by making a sketch that exactly fits the planned mosaic area. Spaces for individual pieces are not drawn in exact detail because colors and ideas may inspire changes as you go along. It is helpful to think of both the design and the background as consisting of broad strokes of color rather than lines because they will be developed chiefly in rows of glass tesserae. If the rows are smooth and flowing, they will give strength and unity to the mosaic design. These rows can be developed in the design. Some areas may depart from a pattern of rows; they are filled with odd-shaped small pieces placed at random, making an interesting contrast to rows of tesserae.

When the pattern is completed, trace it onto the surface prepared for the mosaic. Thicken the lines on both the pattern and the prepared surface by tracing over them with a felt tipped marker. These broad lines represent narrow spaces between glass pieces. Use a light gray marker or pencil for the traced design on the prepared mosaic base because you may make a few changes as you arrange the tesserae. Gray is not likely to show through the glass after it is applied. Black lines are traced over the original pattern. The glass is cut over this pattern. It will be cut into strips that fit between these thick lines; the small tesserae are cut from the strips.

Detail of a 20' X 47' stained glass mosaic. By Glass-art Studio of Phoenix, Arizona. Installed in the Sun-land Mausoleum in Sun City, Arizona.

Some are cut individually to fit into odd spaces. It is well to be flexible and adapt the glass to the design.

To retain smooth lines and the unity of the design, the glass strips should conform closely to the widths of the rows where they are designated in the pattern. It is advisable to read again the section on cutting glass. Remember, too many lines should not be scored on the glass before it is separated. Score and separate each strip, then score and break apart the small glass tesserae individually. If you score a grill-type pattern of lines and then try to separate a lot of little uniform pieces at once, it will only make cutting more difficult, not easier, By cutting them individually from strips of glass, you can angle edges slightly to fit along curves. It is very helpful to examine illustrations of mosaics in magazines and books to see how different mosaic artists worked out their problems by subtly shaping the small tesserae.

The glass pieces for the demonstrated project are washed in detergent water, a few at a time, then rinsed, dried, and *replaced* on the pattern. At this point, care must be taken to avoid mixing up the pieces lest a discouraging amount of time be required to relocate them on the working pattern. The edges of glass mosaic pieces must be either sanded or fired to 1350°F in a small kiln to just blunt the sharp edges but retain shape. All glass colors must be test-fired to find out whether they change color. In testing colors for the illustrated project, it was found that the brown glass fired to opaque black and the orange fired red. The edges of those glass pieces were lightly sanded for the mosaic.

To fire glass tesserae, lay them in their original order on the kiln shelf, which has been coated with sifted kiln wash for a separator. After the pieces are fired, they are replaced on the pattern. If you cannot fire the glass, all cut edges are sanded with fine emery paper, preferably under water, to remove dangerous sharp slivers and corners. Protect your eyes from flying bits. The small table for the project is moved near the tesserae so they can be easily transferred to it before they are epoxied. Changes in the arrangement of the glass design are made before epoxying begins. Once started it must proceed smoothly without interruption. If the border around the planned mosaic area is wood or metal, protect it with masking tape before bonding begins.

Following directions in the section "Bonded Glass," each piece is picked up, epoxied on the back and placed on the table design that has been drawn directly on the table top. Begin with main design features, then work in the lesser areas and the background. Most projects require several mixings of the resin and hardener. Mix only the amount you can use in 30 to 40 minutes, following exactly the directions that accompany the epoxy. Leave a ⅛-to ¼-inch margin all around the edge. It will be filled in with grout. When all the glass is applied, remove the masking tape carefully. Bits of resin that get on the glass must be removed with epoxy solvent on a cloth. Do not let the solvent run between the tesserae. It will weaken the adhesive that holds the glass in place. Leave the work undisturbed overnight. When it is dry, it is time to mix the grout.

All spaces for individual pieces are not drawn in exact detail because ideas may inspire changes as you work. Trace heavy black lines over the drawing to indicate narrow spaces that will be filled with grout after the glass is bonded.

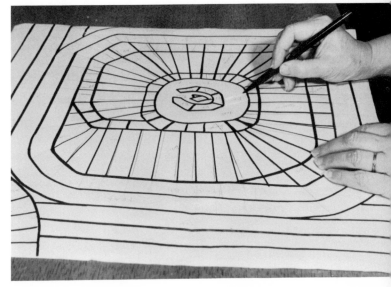

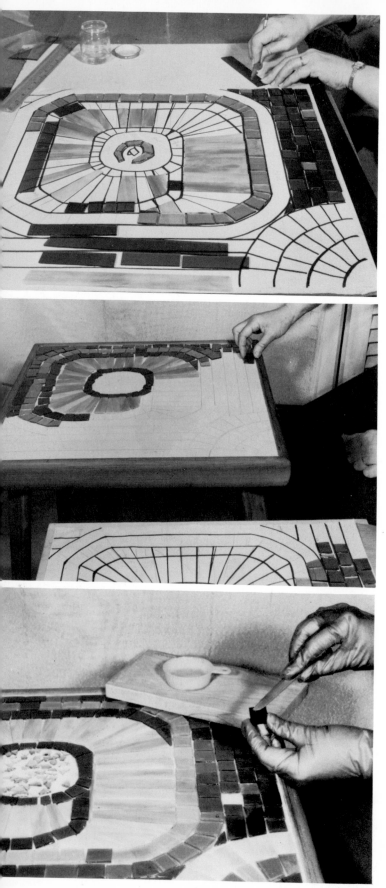

Small tesserae are cut from long strips of glass that are cut to fit between parallel lines in the design. They are positioned on the pattern.

When all the glass is cut, transfer the glass tesserae from the paper drawing to the traced design on the painted white table top so you do not lose them or mix them up.

Mix small amounts of epoxy at a time. Spread a thin coat of adhesive to the back of each glass piece and press it firmly into position on the table top until all are glued.

Thoroughly blend the dry tile grout with coloring powder before you add water, unless you are using it white. A cup of dry white tile grout mixed with brown coloring powder to medium brown was used for the demonstration project. The grouted area is 20 by 20 inches. Color all the dry grout you think is necessary for a project and blend it well; then mix small amounts of it with a water and glue solution (three parts of water to one of glue) to work over a small area at a time. When you have mixed it to toothpaste consistency, let it sit for a few moments and then it should be just about right for working into spaces between the glass pieces. Force it into the cracks with a flexible rubber spatula pressed flat against the glass. Lightly scrape most of the excess grout from the tesserae with the spatula, but do not disturb the grout in the cracks until it has set. Then clean up with damp rags. Do not wait too long before you clean the grouted area completely. If it dries on the glass, it can be stubborn to remove. It can be sprayed *very lightly* with water to assist the cleanup. Cover the mosaic with plastic wrapping sheet for eight hours to assure slow drying that will prevent fine cracks from forming in the grout. When it is quite dry, polish the wood, grout and glass with liquid wax or marble polish.

When the epoxy has dried for 24 hours, mix enough grout and water paste to fill crevices in a limited area at one time. With a very flexible rubber spatula, work it into the cracks and lightly scrape away some of the excess grout. When it is firm but not dry, clean the glass with damp rags. Cover it with plastic wrapping sheet for eight hours to prevent cracks from forming.

After several days of "curing," the mosaic is rubbed with steel wool, and the entire table and mosaic are waxed with liquid wax.

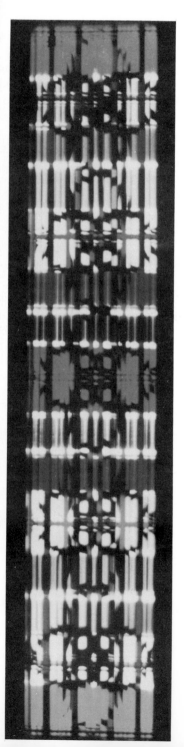

Three-dimensional stained glass. Fredrica H. Fields. Layers of stained glass in many colors in a shadow box panel, 26½″ X 13″. *Photo by Kenneth E. Fields.* (See Fredrica Fields's Work, Section 8).

▶

Layered three-dimensional stained glass panel. Fredrica H. Fields. National Cathedral, Washington, D.C. *Photo by Kenneth E. Fields.*

A SMALL BONDED WINDOW

A sketch is drawn for a small bonded window to be made from antique stained glass bonded to $\frac{3}{16}$-inch plate glass. Three full-scale copies are made, one on heavy paper to be cut into patterns. In measuring for the clear glass base, allow at least ¼ inch around the edge to be free of stained glass so there will be a space for framing the window. When the patterns are cut, space is allowed for grout between each glass shape. Tape one drawing to the table and tape the plate over it, masking off the ¼ inch around the edge. After the glass has been washed, dried, and laid out on the third drawing, it is time to mix just the amount of epoxy you can apply in thirty minutes. Spread a thin coating of adhesive to each glass and press it firmly into position. Make sure the table is level or the glass will likely slide out of position before it can dry. Continue to mix and apply epoxy until all the glass is in place. Clean up the glass with a rag dampened with epoxy solvent and a razor blade, after the epoxy has become rubbery. Do not let the solvent seep into the cracks between glass pieces. When the glass has dried overnight, fill all the cracks with grout. When excess grout has been cleaned away, cover the glass with a plastic sheet for eight hours to prevent cracks from forming in the grout.

A small scale sketch for a bonded window, "Stems and Flowers." Dark areas indicate grouted work.

Three copies are made of the full-scale drawing. Only one border line is required for the bonded window.

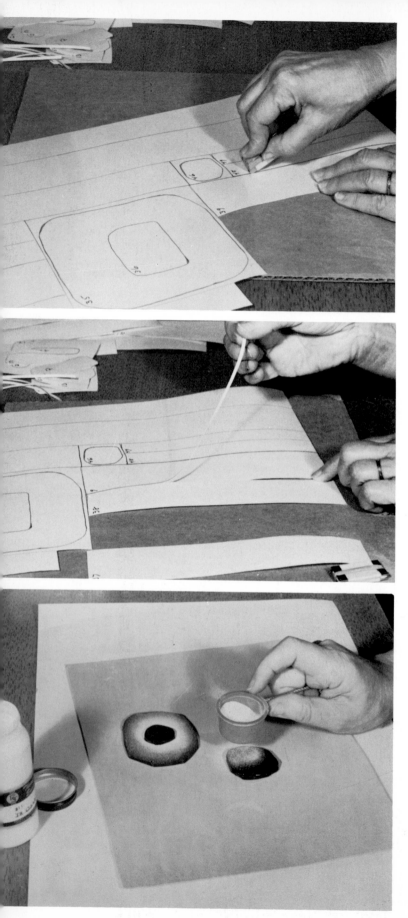

Individual patterns are cut out. Use pattern shears if they are available.

The removed strips leave spaces that indicate where grouting will be applied instead of leads.

Abstract flower shapes will be fused and bonded, both singly and in layers. To facilitate fusion, sift glass flux over the glass before it is fired. (For directions on how to fuse small glass pieces, refer to the section "Fused Glass Wind-chimes.")

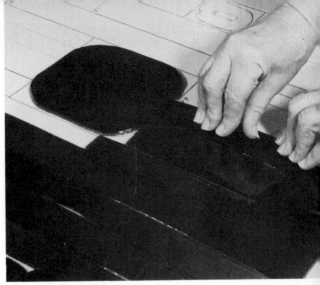

Read again the instructions under "Glass Bonded with Epoxy Resin," before you begin work on a large project. If only one person is bonding the glass, no more than one-fourth of the total amount of glass in this window can be bonded before the epoxy begins to set. Remove the masking tape along the edge as soon as the epoxy becomes rubbery.

The third application of resin begins.

A section of the completed window, STEMS AND FLOWERS.

Faceted glass window. First Presbyterian Church, Bartlesville, Oklahoma. Willet Stained Glass Studios.

FACETED STAINED GLASS

The imaginative use of thick segments of sparkling antique stained glass has formed a major contemporary glass craft in this country and in Europe. It is reminiscent of an old art first developed by the Egyptians and the Byzantines when thick colored glass was the only kind available to them for creating mosaics and windows. Segments of the semi-transparent blocks of glass imbedded in walls and window openings transformed medieval churches from gloomy caverns to jeweled shrines of mysterious beauty. As time passed and glass became thinner, painters covered areas of it with pictorial delineations, hiding the real beauty of the glowing glass colors. Stained glass reached a plateau of development where it remained for centuries.

Near the end of the nineteenth century, French glass artists traveling to ancient shrines "rediscovered" the beauty of simple primitive works. They developed a thick, unusually clear and vibrantly colored stained glass cast into thick slabs that they called "dalles-de-verre" (flagstones of glass). They chipped the glass in a special way to make light reflective, sparkling facets. Soon glass artists in many countries were experimenting with faceted glass. They began to recapture with pure color and symbolic form the emotional and psychological elements of spiritual truths, which they built primarily into religious architecture. Detailed realistic representations are not needed in this mingling of light and color. Sensitive juxtaposition of colors, subtle faceting and expert arrangement of vibrant glass in a contrasting sober matrix, suffice to modify the bold glass forms. When the eye encounters the rich hues in a faceted glass mural wall or window, the viewer does not engage in interpreting the various shapes, colors, and textures of the composition. His emotions become deeply involved with its pervasive spell, stilling any inclination to identify realistic pictorial details.

Glass dalles are made in a wide variety of vibrant and subtle colors developed by modern chemistry. The slabs may be sized 8 by 8 inches to 12 by 12 inches, and ½ to 1 inch thick. Shaped segments of faceted glass can be bonded into panels of cement in warm or moderate climates or interior installations. Weather fluctuations make cement-bonded glass impractical for exterior use in cold or variable climates. Cement shrinks at a different rate than glass in cold temperatures; the glass can loosen. In some instances it has even fallen out of its matrix. Professional craftsmen are bonding faceted glass with a special adhesive usually mixed with sand. The epoxy employed in the demonstration project is Thermoset #16 Epoxy and Hardener, available in several appropriate colors: black, charcoal, limestone, mortar, and adobe. The adhesive is formulated to give structural strength, durability, and weather resistance to interior and exterior slab glass installations. It is easy to to use if the manufacturer's directions are followed exactly.

A predesigned faceted panel usually begins with a color sketch enlarged to a full-size cartoon representing glass segments that will be cut to a pattern. But cutting slab glass requires special tools and skills. Because of the high cost of individual glass slabs, it is recommended that the beginner make his initial projects from broken slab glass segments, available from stained glass suppliers. They are sold by the pound at smaller cost. Select some pieces of the glass that have interesting shapes and arrange them in a composition on a sheet of paper; trace around each glass segment to make a cartoon and a carbon copy for the work drawing.

Before the project begins, all the glass pieces must be washed in hot detergent water, rinsed in warm water, and dried. Four boards are nailed together to make a frame of correct dimensions into which the panel is cast. Varnish the frame's interior surface and seal its inside corners with masking tape. Then rub it with paste wax. The next step is the preparation of the base of the frame. The full-size work drawing, indicating the position of the glass segments for the planned panel, is spread out on a sheet of ¾-inch plywood. Cover it with a transparent parting sheet such as polyethylene sheet, fiberglass laminate, or other plastic. For an initial project, space the glass pieces far enough apart to facilitate pouring the epoxy without dribbling it over the glass. To anchor the wood frame in position over the plastic parting sheet, nail small blocks of wood against the outside of the frame. The nails go into the plywood through the parting sheet and drawing paper that extend beyond the frame. Coat the parting sheet with paste wax.

The bottom of each slab glass segment must be sealed off to prevent epoxy from running underneath it. A material such as latex (Thermoset #529 was used for the demonstration project) acts as both a sealant for the glass and a release agent for the parting sheet and the frame, when the epoxy in the panel has set. Brush some latex over the inside of the wooden frame; then paint the bottom of each glass piece with the latex before you set it inside the frame in its designated position on the parting sheet. When all the glass is in place, pour a very thin layer of latex over the plastic parting sheet between glass pieces. To keep the glass clean, wear gloves if you must touch it. After 24 hours, if the latex is dry, it is time to prepare the epoxy resin and hardener. If any glass pieces are deeply faceted around their top edge, you may fill in the facets temporarily with putty to shield them from the epoxy. It can be dug out when the epoxy has set. If you should see a slight buckling of the plastic parting sheet after the latex is dry, do not be dismayed. It may impart a shallow ripple to the surface of the epoxy matrix between glass pieces that can be interesting and attractive. The shallow buckling is caused by air trapped beneath the plastic parting sheet. Some craftsmen pierce the plastic sheet in several places to release the air as the poured epoxy settles.

Epoxy resin is always supplied with a hardener as a unit. They must be mixed together thoroughly. If you have access to a paint shaking mixer, use it as a good blending device, but remember, the epoxy begins to activate as soon as it is blended with its hardener! If you must travel some distance to use a mixer, it is best to forget it! The epoxy compound can be mixed by hand. Should you plan to mix less than the entire amount in the container, the resin and the hardener must be mixed in exactly the same proportions specified in the manufacturer's instructions. A can containing the correct amount of hardener is supplied with each container of epoxy resin. Space is provided in the container for the hardener to be mixed in the same can. It is simple to combine the entire amount of compound for one pouring. An additional project can be planned at the same time should you blend the entire amount of epoxy and then discover you have a surplus left over. Once the ingredients are mixed, they cannot be stored for future use. Be sure the pouring table is level; the slightest slant will cause the glass pieces to slide gently out of place. The epoxy levels out completely, although slowly, so take care not to pour so much that it runs over the shorter glass.

The resin and hardener for the demonstrated project, charcoal gray Thermoset #116 Resin and Hardener, was hand-mixed with a stout stick for five minutes. It was scraped down the sides of the container and *stirred from the bottom up* continually, which brought up very thick dark sandy material. When you first begin to stir the thick mixture, you may have some misgivings about being able to pour it smoothly. Do not be too concerned. Once the thin hardener is added to it and blended vigorously for five minutes, it acquires a wonderful texture and pourable viscosity that will make you marvel at the manufacturer's skill! Be sure to stir it from the bottom up, and do not mix it longer than the time specified on the container.

For the demonstration project, several kinds of pouring vessels were considered in order to find one that could be easily manipulated by the novice. A clean half-gallon milk carton was selected. It was partly filled for each pouring, then it was refilled. You can control a thin stream of the mix by squeezing a corner of the container to make a spout for pouring the compound into narrow spaces between the glass. Pour it to a level approximately ⅝ inch thick. If you inadvertently spill some of it on the glass, remove it with a cloth dampened with epoxy solvent. Should you want a sand-finished surface, sift sand evenly over the setting epoxy *15 to 20 minutes after* the casting to prevent too much sand from sinking out of sight into the matrix. If too much sand sinks into it, the level of the epoxy may rise and cover some of the glass.

In order to use up surplus epoxy that might be left over when the entire gallon container of epoxy was blended, an extra free-form panel was prepared at the time the rectangular demonstration project was planned. Heavy waxed linoleum was employed for a frame instead of wood. To make this kind of frame, set a strip of linoleum on edge with the smooth side facing in, and bend it to the desired shape. Wrap and fasten heavy twine around it, then press a roll of moist clay into the outside angle where the linoleum meets the plastic topped base. Follow the same preparatory procedure outlined for the larger panel. A short length of copper pipe ⅞ inch wide and ¾ inch long was set into the latex release agent one-half inch from the edge of the linoleum strip at the time glass pieces were positioned, to provide for a hanging device.

Panels cast with this kind of special epoxy resin should cure for 24 hours at normal room temperature. After that time, the latex sealant is stripped from it. Allow several days before installation. If a faceted glass panel will be set into an exterior wall, it should be secured on setting blocks (such as lead blocks) with enough clearance on all sides to provide for expansion and contraction during changes in the weather. It should be sealed with permanently flexible caulking compound. In a construction where many panels are stacked, adequate reinforcement must be provided, of course.

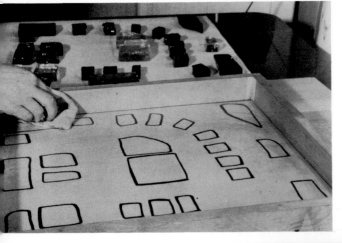

A full-size drawing is laid out on a sheet of plywood and covered with a transparent parting sheet. The wood frame is anchored over it. The base and the inside of the frame are coated with hard paste wax.

Liquid latex brushed over the inside of the wood frame provides a release agent for the epoxy panel.

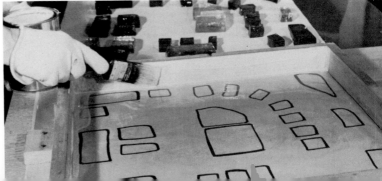

The bottom of each glass is coated with latex before it is set in place. The latex turns translucent and light tan as it dries.

When all glass is positioned, the thin latex is poured over the parting sheet between glass pieces. If it is poured over 1/8'' thick it may crack as it dries.

A half-gallon milk carton provides an excellent pouring vessel for the heavy dark epoxy that is poured over the dry latex.

The top of the carton is cut so it slants away from one corner, which provides a good spout for pouring into narrow spaces.

An oval of linoleum with clay pressed around it provides the mold frame for a smaller panel.

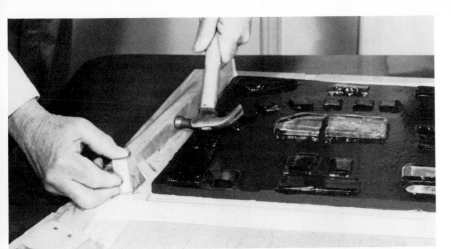

When the resin has set, the frame is knocked loose from the panel. Notice the thin sheet of latex pulling away from the wood.

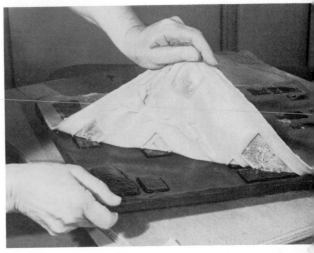

The latex release sheet offers no resistance when it is pulled away from the panel.

One completed panel for a divider.

THREE FACES. Old Dominion Stained Glass Company. The black epoxy matrix gives dynamic definition to this simple faceted glass design.

CREATION. Laws Stained Glass Studio. Faceted glass in a black epoxy matrix.

Faceted walls, windows, and dividers have gained phenomenal acceptance by architects, artists, and laymen alike. Reflection, refraction, and transmission of light in a mélange of vibrant color produces emotion of depth and power particularly suited to religious architecture. In our time, however, faceted glass is not limited to ecclesiastical settings, but it enriches the durable planes and volumes of modern secular architecture everywhere with shimmering color and lasting beauty.

Faceted window. Chapel of Warren State Hospital, Warren, Pennsylvania. Willet Stained Glass Studios.

Jan selects glass dalles. Each slab of glass is numbered according to color.

Jan Ozog designs a faceted lumiere (design in full color) for the Willet Stained Glass Studios.

Mike Caputo patterns a faceted glass cartoon at the Willet Stained Glass Studios.

James Harris chops a knobbed (scored) glass dalle. The individual pattern is held against the glass. Willet Stained Glass Studios.

Detail of James Harris chopping.

Pouring epoxy in a faceted window section at the Willet Stained Glass Studios.

Jan Ozog pours resin for a gemmaux panel. A mélange of richly colored glass segments are imbedded in transparent resin for this method.

Faceted glass crucifixion. Saint Mark's Lutheran Church, Glastonbury, Connecticut. Willet Stained Glass Studios.

BURNING BUSH. Willet Studio. Designed for and installed in Temple Shalom, Levittown, Pennsylvania. Faceted glass.

Kiln-fired laminated glass suspension. R. Bruce Laughlin.

4
Fired Glass

GLASSES FOR KILN-FIRING

WINDOW Glass. Colorless transparent sheet glass has many uses besides windowmaking. But glass sources know just what kind of glass is indicated when you ask for it as window glass. It is available in single-strength ($\frac{1}{16}$ inch), double-strength ($\frac{1}{8}$ inch), and in $\frac{3}{16}$- and $\frac{1}{4}$-inch thicknesses. Glass pieces that will be laminated together should be made by the same manufacturer. If you are not sure that they are of identical composition, test-fire a lamination of small pieces. If they do not fracture upon cooling, it may be assumed they are identical. Should you want to laminate circles or ovals before you become adept at cutting glass, or if you are pressed for time, you can have them cut where you purchase glass. For initial projects, single-strength glass is suitable for pieces up to six inches wide in one-layer projects. Pieces of wider diameter should be cut from glass that is double-strength, again specifically one-layer compositions. Two layers of single-strength glass are satisfactory for laminations up to 12 inches across.

Plate Glass. Window glass and plate glass are sold in the same thicknesses. Because of its strength, clarity, and freedom from imperfections, it is useful as a base for bonded assemblages. Plate glass is sometimes very hard and may tend to separate erratically when it is cut. It is also more expensive than the same thickness in window glass. For standard use, the window glass serves very well for fired projects. A few of the colorless sheet glasses tend to devitrify when they are fired; within a certain temperature range they crystallize if they are held too long at a sustained high temperature (usually just below the liquefication point). This temperature is usually reached only when glass is cast, blown, or otherwise manipulated by the experienced craftsman. A complex technical explanation is not in the scope of this book. But it is well to know that a glass that tends to devitrify will acquire a frosted effect. It may be considered desirable in some instances, of course.

Stained Glass. Antique stained glass varies in thickness in each sheet of glass. It can be used successfully for bending or slumping in single sheets. The results of laminating or of fusing together different colors of stained glass cannot be accurately predicted. Many colors are not compatible when they are fused together because of differences in their composition resulting from their various metallic oxide colorants. Reds, oranges, and red golds are not usually successful when they are fused to other colors, although they may sometimes fuse to one another. On rare occasions a colored glass may not remain fused to another piece of the same color. But very lovely objects are made of single sheets of stained glass bent into shape over a mold. These characteristics of antique glass apply to cathedral glass as well as antique, except that cathedral glass is rolled between steel rollers when it is still hot and flexible. It is sold in ⅛-inch even thickness. Various stained glass colors should be test fired before they are used in fired projects. (For more on stained glasses, see the section "Stained Glass.")

Preformed Shapes. Bottles, fruit jars, glass plates, old glass ornaments, ashtrays, and combinations of these and other preformed glass objects are usually easy to find and cost very little. Much molded old glass is soft and fires to a sparkling clarity. As with any material, whether or not it is excellent depends upon the manner of its treatment. It can be fired on a mold like any flat glass.

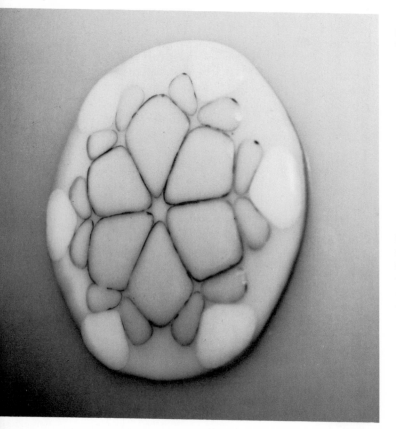

Fused glass. R. Bruce Laughlin. The panel is deep pink with yellow triangular shapes around the edge.

▶

Fused glass. BoBo Zinn. The smaller circle of glass with added small glass shapes was covered with a combination of blue and green glass ices and opaque enamels. It was fired flat separately on the kiln shelf until glowing red and molten. Edges were manipulated and pleated with a firing tool while in the kiln. The clear glass background panel was fired to attach the hanger and round glass edges. The two panels were cemented together with R-TV glue. *Photo by Drew Henery.*

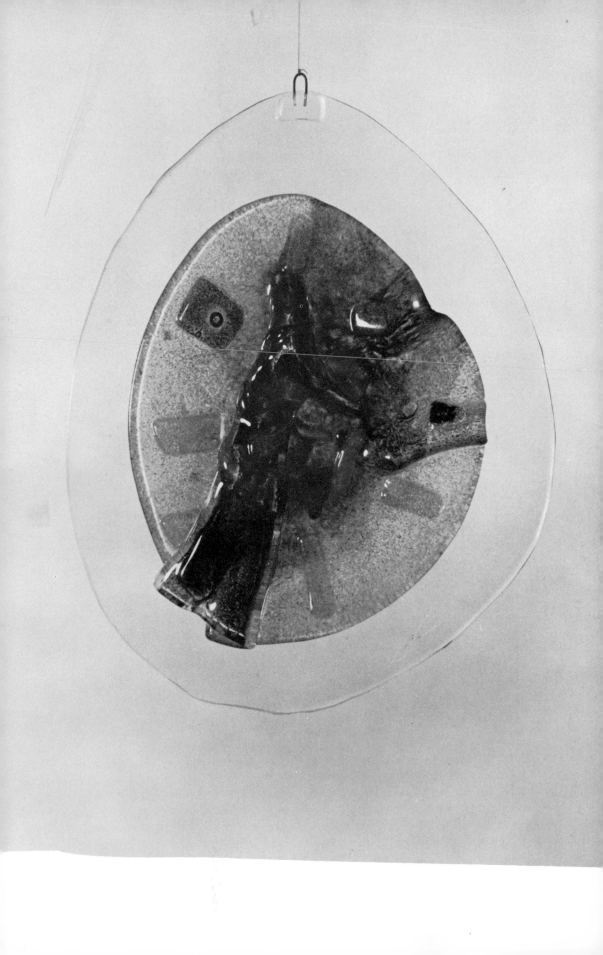

Fused glass. R. Bruce Laughlin. Circular panel with applied shapes and colors fused in one firing with nichrome wire hanger.

KILNS

Individual kilns do not all fire the same; specific firing results are therefore difficult to forecast for all kilns. The kiln-fired glass projects in this book were fired in either a front-loading electric enameling kiln, 12 by 12 by 7½ inches high, or a top-loading electric ceramic kiln, 13½ by 14½ inches. Kilns such as these, which have pyrometers and temperature controls, will fire almost any kind of glass fusing or bending projects for the average craftsman who has a small studio. The front loader is wired around the walls and across the floor. Ideally, a glass-firing kiln is also wired in the door. But if you refrain from opening the door or vents after the temperature has climbed to 1,000°F, until firing is completed, even without door-wiring, glass can be fired successfully. In a front-loading kiln, glass pieces should be set back from the door a few inches; the kiln's interior temperature may be cooler near the door, especially if the door is opened during the firing process. The edges of the glass nearest the door may be somewhat angular when the rest of the glass has fired to maturity, if positioned too near the door.

For accurate glass firing, the kiln should be equipped with a pyrometer. Kiln switches are operated several times during one glass firing. The use of a number of pyrometric cones to indicate different heating adjustments for one firing is awkward; it permits only partial temperature control. The serious glass craftsman, whether amateur or professional, will make the extra expenditure required for this important piece of equipment. Accurate temperature control is imperative for the successful firing of any glass.

KILN FURNITURE

High-fired ceramic kiln shelves, usually available in square, round, and half-round shapes and in different sizes, retain heat for quite a while longer than the glass, after the switches are turned off. It is advisable to elevate molds from the shelf with short kiln posts, sections of insulation brick, or a square of acoustical insulation board treated as described under "Molds for Firing Glass."

Whatever elevation prop is used should support the mold level, or the glass will bend at an angle.

To keep insulation brick posts from crumbling, dip them in a solution of equal parts of water and sodium silicate (water glass), dry them and fire them to 1500°F on a kiln shelf sifted with dry kiln wash for a separator.

MOLDS FOR FIRING GLASS

Refractory molds are a requirement for fusing, bending, or contouring glass. The glass is positioned on top of the mold and both are put into a cool kiln. After the kiln switches are turned on, the heat is increased gradually until the glass fuses or bends to fit the contours of the mold. Glass that will be fused flat can be fired directly on the kiln shelf, but this method becomes awkward if you fire glass continually over a period of time. Glass can be fired flat on sections of Marinite, Armstrong Ceramiguard, or other fireproof acoustical board. These fireproof sheets must be heat treated in the kiln before they can be employed as supports for firing glass. They have been low-fired, and are soft and porous.

To strengthen the insulation boards, fire them with the rough side down to 1600°– 1800°F on a regular kiln shelf that has been covered with a coating of kiln wash. The kiln and the room must be ventilated for the preliminary firing of these insulation sheets. They give off pungent fumes during the first firing that could cloud the glass if they are not prefired. Fire them for one hour at *low* with the door ajar ½ inch. Then turn the switch to *high* for ½ hour with the door still ajar. At this time the increased temperature will bring fumes and smoke from the insulation board. A door or window must be opened so

smoke can disperse during this first firing. The smooth white top side of the board will turn to a light caramel color temporarily, then it will turn white again. After ½ hour, close the kiln door and continue firing to about 1600°F with the switches still on *high*. Finally turn off the kiln and let it cool naturally. The ceramic material in these boards can cause them to crack if the kiln door is opened while they are still hot or if they are not fired perfectly flat on the kiln shelf. When they have cooled, fill all the pits by rubbing a paste of whiting (calcium carbonate) and water into them. After the boards are fired, they will be firm and somewhat brittle; but if they are handled with reasonable care, they should give good service. In addition they are lightweight and inexpensive. Sift kiln wash over them as a separator.

One of the most common kinds of material for making shaped molds is ready-prepared white sculpture clay (cone 04) bought moist from the supplier. The molds are fired to cone 08, which leaves the clay somewhat porous and less likely to crack when glass is fired on it. Simple greenware shapes can be used for molds if there are no undercut details that may prevent the fired bent glass from releasing from the clay.

One of the most common kinds of mold material is white sculpture clay. This is a 25-pound plastic bag of the clay as it comes ready-to-use from the supplier.

Roll out some clay between two sticks about ¼'' thick.

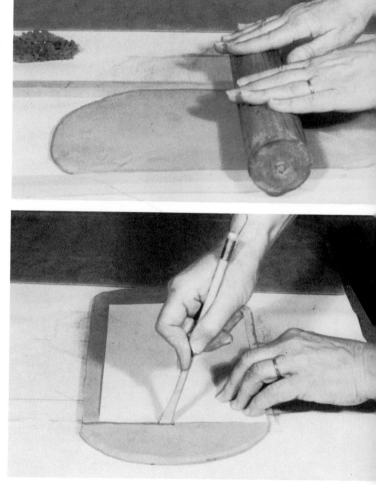

Lay out a cardboard pattern the size and shape of the mold you plan and cut the clay around it.

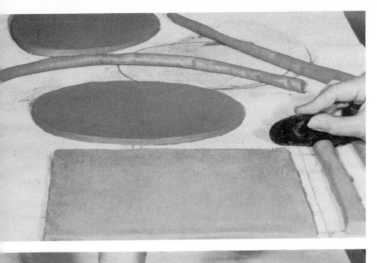

Roll thick clay coils that will prop up the rim of each slab that will become a mold.

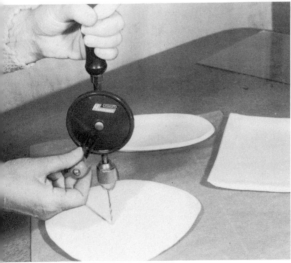

When the clay shape has become slightly firm but not stiff, lift up each edge and prop it into position with coils. Do not remove them until the tray has become leather hard or it will slowly flatten out before it is dry.

As soon as the clay is bone dry, the molds are fired to cone 08. Several small holes are drilled in the center and along the base edge of each mold before they are used.

Rub whiting (calcium carbonate) over the surface of each mold to fill in any rough spots.

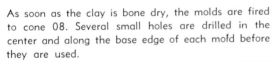

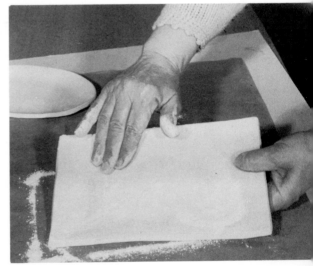

Push whiting out of each clogged hole with a toothpick so air can pass through when glass slumps into the mold. Otherwise, a huge bubble may be formed by trapped air.

A piece of red stained glass is cut to fit the shape of a free-form mold. Clear glass flux is sifted over it very lightly to make a fine texture in the glass when it is fired.

Kiln wash was sifted over the mold for a separator before the glass was lowered into position. The glass must not extend beyond the edge of the mold.

The glowing red of ruby antique glass with its natural streaks of lighter and darker color could not be improved with surface designing.

Certain powdered castable refractories such as Kastolite (or other castable refractories), used for chimney and furnace linings, make excellent molds for glass bending. This kind of material is cast over a model of the desired shape. Place a form such as a bowl upside down on a square of ¾-inch plywood board. Snip off the heads of some tacks or brads and drive them into the board all around the bowl's perimeter to hold it in position. A strip of linoleum should be cut at least an inch wider than the deepest measurement of the model and a little longer than its circumference. Wrap the strip, smooth side in and standing on edge, around the model and headless tacks with the ends of the linoleum lapped. Tie it temporarily with string wound around it while you drive long slim nails all around close against it. Brush vegetable oil over the outside of the inverted model so the mold will release from it easily.

When the model is ready, it is time to mix the Kastolite. Because this material is composed of small variably sized particles, over a period of time the finest dustlike grains sift to the bottom of the bag container. The entire dry bagful must be mixed thoroughly before it is used. To make stronger molds,

blend in a cupful of powdered alumina to a 2½-gallon bucketful of the dry material, then mix it with water to lava consistency. Scoop it over the top of the greased model, pushing it well down the sides. When the mold enclosure is half filled, lift the plywood base at one end and *gently* rap it down against the table several times to bring air bubbles to the surface. Sprinkle a little dry Kastolite over the surface to absorb moisture rising to the top. Add some of the dry material to the remainder of the mixture, stir it well, and fill the mold to the top with this dryer mixture. Rap the plywood again and soak up surface water with layers of paper toweling. The mold should set for at least 24 hours without being disturbed; then carefully remove the linoleum strip and let the mold dry another 12 hours. Remember that the mold is fragile until it is fired. Remove the model and put the mold into a cool kiln with its door open about an inch; turn switches to *low* for an hour to drive off remaining moisture or oil. When the door has been closed, turn the switches to *high* and fire to 1400°–1500°F. After the kiln is turned off, let it cool before you remove the mold.

Drill some air holes in the mold with a

hand drill. They will prevent large bubbles of air from becoming trapped under sagging glass. Seal the mold by brushing it generously inside and outside with a thin solution of sodium silicate (water glass). To fill all the pits in the top of the mold, rub a paste of whiting and water into them and wipe a thin film of the paste over the surface. This paste will also clog the drilled air holes; to reopen them, pierce each one with a needle or tooth-pick. The mold should be refired to 800°F before the first time glass is bent over it.

Unusual and exciting shapes in bent glass are formed over nichrome wire, high-fire clay stilts, plate pins, insulation brick forms, and other materials that can withstand heat high enough to bend glass. Molds made from these materials are all coated with a separator such as kiln wash before glass is bent over them.

Slumped or sagged glass. BoBo Zinn. An eight-inch circle was decorated by brushing strokes of enameling gum on the glass, sifting on several enamel colors, then tapping off excess. It was slumped into a mold. *Photo by Drew Henery.*

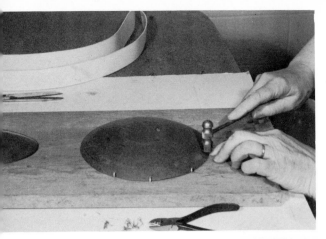

A raised metal form is the model for casting a mold. Place any bowl form upside down on a square of ¾'' plywood board. Snip off the heads of some tacks or brads and drive them into the board around the bowl's edge to hold it in position.

A strip of linoleum is wrapped, smooth side in, around the model and headless tacks. Linoleum ends are lapped.

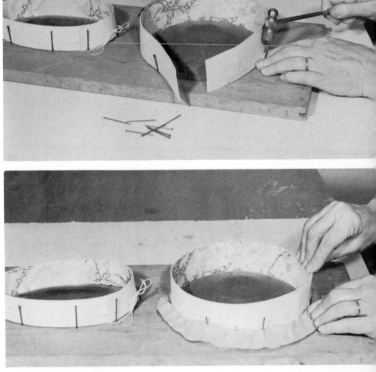

Drive long slim nails all around the outside of the linoleum and press a roll of clay against it. Brush or pour vegetable oil over the outside of the inverted model so the mold will release from it later.

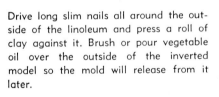

Scoop the mold mixture over the top of the greased model.

Sprinkle dry Kastolite over the surface of the mold mixture to absorb moisture rising to the top.

Soak up surface moisture with layers of paper.

Rap the plywood against the table occasionally to level the Kastolite mix and bring bubbles of air to the top.

After 24 hours, remove the linoleum strip and the model. Let the mold continue to dry in a warm place. Place it in a cool kiln to fire at 1400°–1500°F.

When the cooled mold has been removed from the kiln, bore several holes in it and fill all pinholes by rubbing the mold surface with whiting. Push whiting out of each bored hole with a toothpick. Sift it with fresh kiln wash each time it is used.

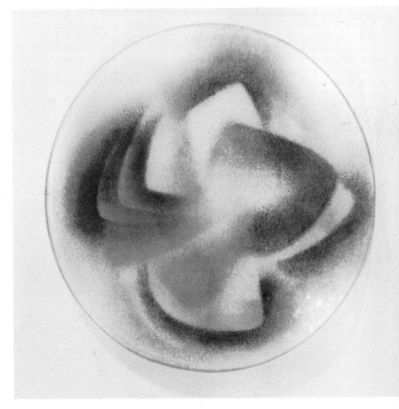

A circle of single-strength window glass with a soft-edged stencil pattern of low-fusing glass ice and enamels was slumped into the mold in one firing. The heat was brought to 1350°F to fire the colors and blunt the edges of the form.

KILN WASH

The ceramic shelves in any kiln are given at least three coats of kiln wash to protect them from drippings of glaze, enamel, or melted glass. Mix the dry kiln wash (equal parts of kaolin and flint) with water to thin cream consistency. Brush the shelf first with plain water, then in quick long strokes brush on three even coats of the kiln wash crosswise to one another. For best results, let the shelf dry completely and slowly for a day or two in a warm (not hot) place. When the shelf is in use, if enamel, glaze, or glass drippings fall to the shelf and melt, they can be cleaned away easily. Just scrape off the spots and patch the scraped areas with additional kiln wash.

Dry kiln wash sifted through 80-mesh screen is an excellent separator between glass and any mold used for fusing or bending glass. It leaves a fine texture in the glass and protects the mold from molten glass that could otherwise stick to it. After every two or three firings, brush off the used kiln wash and sift a new layer over the mold.

MAKING A KILN WASH SIFTER

A practical sifter for applying kiln wash as a separator can be made from a 13-ounce tuna can (not the regular smaller size). Clean it thoroughly with detergent water, rinse it and dry it. Remove both ends of the can. Cut a circle of 80-mesh brass sieve cloth a little larger in diameter than the can, turn up the edge, and solder it to the *rim* of the tuna can. It will likely not adhere to the side of the can, which usually has a coating that does not accept most solder. Use either low-fusing paste solder or 60/40 solid core solder that must be fluxed. (For the soldering process, see "Soldering" in the stained glass section.)

When the sifter has been soldered, wash it well in detergent water to remove any oil from the solder flux, then press narrow self-adhering plastic tape firmly around the edge of the brass sieve cloth to cover rough wire ends that could scratch your fingers. Use a soft dry two-inch nylon paintbrush to apply the powdered kiln wash by whisking it back and forth to push the powder through the sifter. Move the sifter around above the mold surface as you brush a fine sifting over every part of the mold surface.

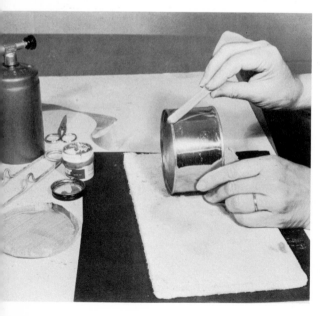

Low-fusing paste solder called Fast (trade name) is spread along the rim of the tuna can. Notice the circle of brass sieve-cloth with its edge turned up ready for soldering to the can.

Spread more paste solder on the edge over the sieve cloth, which has been positioned on the rim of the can.

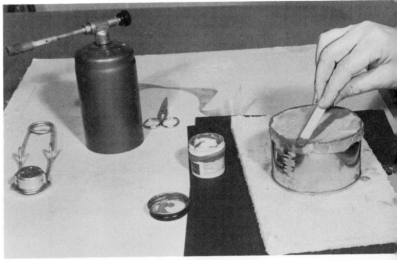

The brass sieve material is held tightly against the rim with a ni-chrome rod as the torch moves around the edge and melts the solder. Let the solder cool before you disturb it.

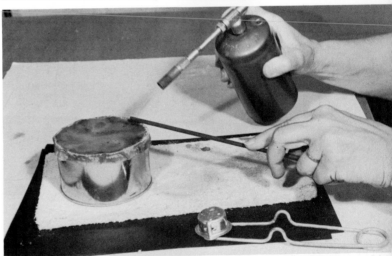

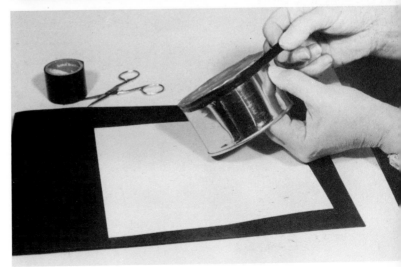

Press narrow self-adhering plastic tape firmly over the wire ends that could scratch your fingers.

Use a soft nylon paintbrush to whisk the kiln wash through the sifter in a thin layer over any surface on which glass will be fired.

Slumped glass bowl. R. Bruce Laughlin. Laminated and decorated with glass enamels. (See section ''Bubbles in Laminated Glass.'')

THE FIRING SCHEDULE

General kiln-firing procedures are given here for fusing glass flat. Specific requirements for bent or sagged glass are discussed separately. When glass is ready for firing, it is placed in a cool kiln on its prepared mold or shelf. Position it away from the kiln door and from the electric elements. The temperature controls are turned to *low* and the door is left ajar for a gentle preheating period of two hours or longer, depending upon the size and the number of pieces to be fired. By the end of that period, the temperature should be approximately 400° to 500°F. In a large fully loaded kiln, the preliminary heating period can be several hours.

All glass firing requires the kiln to be vented until the temperature reaches approximately 950°F (or cone 022). Atmospheric moisture in the kiln, the mold, and in the room, as well as gases from chemicals in materials fired into the glass, can cloud the heating glass if they cannot escape from the kiln quickly. By venting the kiln while it is heating to approximately 950°F, you can assure that all these gases escape from the kiln. This means opening a peephole and leaving the door or lid ajar. To vent a top-loading kiln during the preliminary heating period, prop its lid open about ½ inch and leave the lower peephole open. The door of a front-loading kiln is left open ½ inch. After two or more hours on *low,* turn the switches to *high* and adjust the kiln door to be only slightly ajar until the temperature reaches 950°F. In a top-loading kiln, the lid props must be lowered so there is only a slight opening. Peepholes are closed. Protect your eyes, face, hands, and arms from the intense heat that emanates from the top loader while you are changing lid props.

In addition to allowing fumes and moisture to escape readily, venting slows down the temperature rise and deters the hazard of glass breakage in a kiln that tends to heat too fast. The *medium* switch is rarely used because in many kilns it turns off half the elements which can cause uneven heating that sets up stresses in glass. When the pyrometer indicates approximately 950°F, close the kiln vents and door. After that time, maintain a close watch over the rising temperature. Check the glass visually from time to time, beginning at 1200°F. When the glass edges are gently rounded and the glass becomes red, flat glass is mature. This will occur at a lower temperature for stained glass than for window glass. When the temperature reaches 1400°F, if you are firing window glass (1300°F for stained glass), turn off the switches and vent the kiln for a few moments. Venting the kiln at this time prevents a continued rise in temperature that may result from heat stored in the kiln walls even after it has been turned off.

After two or three minutes, close the vents again and let the kiln cool to the annealing point of the glass you are firing, or to 950°–1000°F if you do not know the exact annealing range of your particular glass. Then turn the kiln switches on again to low and keep all the vents closed. Hold the temperature between 950° and 1000° for at least an hour or longer to anneal, then let the kiln cool slowly. (An important detailed explanation of the cooling cycle of glass and of annealing continues in the following paragraphs.)

ANNEALING GLASS

Glass has a cooling cycle as well as a firing cycle. If strain, which may cause fracture, is to be avoided, this cycle must be followed. Most kiln-fired materials expand somewhat as their temperature rises and contract as it falls. Glass undergoes this normal thermal expansion and contraction, and in addition, above a certain *transformation* temperature, it undergoes coincidentally a second unique *configurational* change. An intermolecular rearrangement of glass atoms that takes place creates a less open structure in the glass. The change continues at a rate set by the viscosity of the glass as it heats.

No kiln heats evenly throughout. Since most glass is a poor conductor of heat, when the temperature rises in the kiln, warm and cool areas of the glass expand unevenly, causing uneven stresses to form throughout the glass. If the kiln is shut off immediately after firing, the cooling glass will shrink unevenly as it becomes more viscous. Shrinkage is arrested first in the more rapidly cooled areas. Viscosity increases unevenly as the temperature continues to descend, until the intricate internal stresses have become fixed and rigid throughout the glass. The scientific reasons for this behavior of glass are complex. A complete understanding of them is not required of the glass artist, but there should be an awareness that glass does react to high temperature in this manner and that rapidly cooled glass becomes brittle and tends to fracture easily some time after removal from the kiln. This tendency can be controlled by a simple heat treatment called "annealing."

Annealing stabilizes movement within cooling glass so stresses are relieved. As the kiln cools, maintenance of a controlled slow and even temperature gradient (rate of descent) in the hot glass, between certain upper and lower temperature limits known as the *annealing range,* allows time for both configurational and thermal changes to take place. This heat soaking spreads the heat evenly throughout the pliant glass form until flowing glass molecules can gradually realign themselves in an orderly fashion. Strain and brittleness are relieved. The highest point in the annealing range is called the *annealing point;* the lowest temperature is the *strain point.* (Some specific temperatures are given later.) Glass that has cooled without being annealed can and should be reheated above the annealing point and then annealed.

When the temperature has descended to approximately 1000°F, or to the annealing point if it is known, the switches are turned to *low* to hold the temperature stationary for about an hour or longer, according to the kiln load and the size of individual glass objects. Then the switches are turned off. Vents are closed tight during this important period so cooling proceeds slowly and evenly through the annealing range until the temperature descends to 650°F. After that point it can cool more rapidly to room temperature before the glass is removed from the kiln. The rate of descent through the annealing range should be about *20°F every seven minutes* for glass up to ¼ inch thick, and more slowly for large or thick pieces. Two or three layers of glass fused together should be allowed a temperature decrease as slow as *20°F every 10 to 12 minutes* of annealing time. If the temperature drops too fast when your kiln is turned off, switches must be turned back to *low* for five to eight minutes from time to time to slow it down.

The annealing range of different glasses varies as the coefficient (rate or measure) of their expansion varies. The annealing range of stained glass from one manufacturer is 1000°F to 700°F; the annealing range for most window glass falls somewhere between 1070°F and 934°F. It is clear that these different glasses, if fused together, would fracture some time after fusion takes place because they expand and contract at different rates. Temperatures of the annealing range of a specific glass may be obtained from the manufacturer. However, if you cannot get this information, you can determine the rate yourself with a simple test firing. Support a piece of the glass, 6 inches by 1 inch, between two insulation brick posts (across their tops) placed in the kiln so you can observe them through the peephole. Turn the switches to *high.* When the kiln temperature nears 900°F, begin checking the glass closely. The moment a very slight bending of the glass begins, note the exact temperature indicated. Subtract 50°F from that number and you will have the approximate annealing point or top limit of the annealing range of that glass.

FUSED GLASS WINDCHIMES *

Long segments of fused stained glass with silver wire hangers make a colorful set of windchimes that are easy to form. Cut the glass into long rectangular and triangular shapes, two for each chime. When all the planned pieces are cut out, washed and dried, prepare lengths of either nichrome or fine silver wire, 18- or 20-gauge, by curving the ends with small round-nosed jewelry pliers or other shaping tool. Then bend the wires double to make hanging loops for suspending the chimes. Flatten the wire ends gently with a small hammer. The wire ends will be laminated between the top ends of the glass chime layers. Brush each completed wire hanger with alcohol or acetone to remove all traces of soil that could prevent fusion of the glass laminated over them.

Flat molds on which the chimes will be fused are sliced from soft insulation brick with a fine-toothed hacksaw. The top surface of each brick section is rubbed gently with whiting (calcium carbonate) to fill in the pores of the brick and make a smooth surface, as well as to provide a separator between the glass and the insulation brick. It will also prevent the glass from melting into the brick when the kiln is fired. Finally, sift a layer of kiln wash over the whiting. When the glass segments, the wire hangers, and the sections of insulation brick have been prepared, it is time to assemble everything ready for the kiln.

Each chime will be put together on a separate section of brick. Sift clear glass enamel *flux* over the top surface of the *bottom glass segment* of each chime and position it on a section of the prepared brick. Flux will assist the glass fusing process. Pick up one of the wire hangers with tweezers and position it on one end of the glass so the loop extends beyond it. Hold it in place with the

small tweezers while a second glass shape, cut from the same color of glass, is positioned on top of the wire hanger. The edges of some of the glass chimes may be offset very slightly for an interesting variation. The small offset glass edge should not slump over the edge of the glass beneath it if the heat is turned off at the indicated temperature.

If you want to fuse different stained glass colors together, you will find some colors do not remain fused but crack apart some time after the glass cools; the different oxides and other chemicals that determine stained glass colors result in differences in expansion and contraction as the glass heats and cools, or even when draughts in the room drift over the glass some time after it has fired and cooled. Glasses colored with similar oxides, such as blues, greens, and turquoises are less likely to crack apart when they are fused together. But colors should be test-fired before they are used in an important fused glass project.

When all the glass chimes with their wire hangers in place are assembled on the insulation bricks ready for firing, they are positioned in the cool kiln. Switches are turned to *low*. The door or lid is left open ½ inch to allow fumes and any moisture to escape. After an hour of venting (for these small shapes), the switches are turned to *high* until 950°F is reached, when vents are closed. The best way to check the progress of fused glass is to observe it visually. The differences in kilns, kinds and sizes of glass forms, and other possible factors make firing times variable. Begin checking when the kiln temperature reaches 1200°F; when the edges of the glass are rounded, switches are turned off and the kiln is vented immediately to halt further heat rise. After three minutes of venting, close vents and let the kiln cool slowly, following the annealing procedure as outlined earlier.

When the kiln has cooled completely and the chimes are removed, if some residue of

* From an article by the author that appeared in *Ceramics Monthly*.

whiting and kiln wash still clings to the glass, sponge it off carefully with warm water. A piece of striated weathered wood makes a support for these windchimes whose long glass strips make a pattern of vertical striations. Colors for the chimes are blue, green, purple, and amber. Fishline cords strung through the silver wire loops are tied to small staples driven into the back of the weathered wooden support. Touch a drop of glue to each cord knot to ensure it against unraveling when wind moves the chimes. The wooden support can be hung with chains or leather thongs.

Slice sections of soft insulation brick to make flat molds for fusing the chimes.

The top of each brick section is rubbed with whiting to fill pores and provide a separator. Sift a thin film of kiln wash over it.

Position the wire on one end of the lower glass piece and hold it there with tweezers while the second glass is placed on top of it.

Fishline cords strung through the wire loops are tied to small staples driven into the back of a wood support.

Sponge off any residue of kiln wash that clings to the fired glass.

The completed windchimes are green, blue, purple, and amber, suspended from weathered wood.

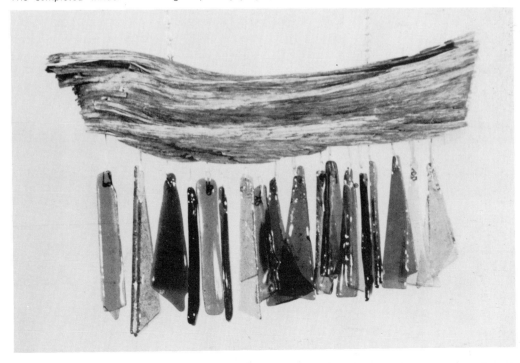

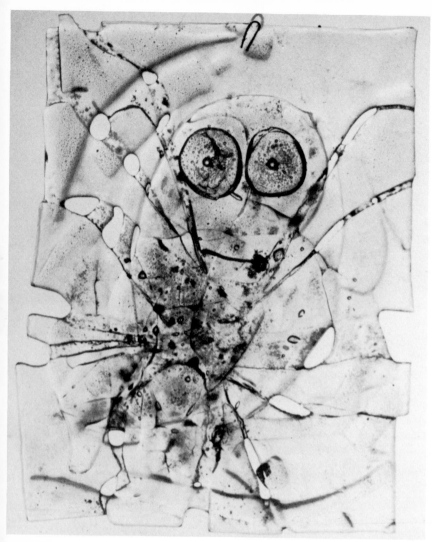

Owl panel. Glenda Davis. Three layers of fragments and sprinklings of transparent green, yellow, and tan glass ices and enamels are fused in one firing.

Fused pendants. Glenda Davis. Clear window glass fragments laminated to glass backgrounds and colored with glass enamels.

BENT AND LAMINATED GLASS

Bent glass is fired over a three-dimensional mold to a temperature at which glass softens, bends, and takes on the contours of the mold. A fired glass object made from two or more glass pieces fused flat or bent together with some decorative material encased between them is *laminated*. Correct firing procedures are a requirement for successfully fused, bent, or laminated glass. A variation of more than 25° from the ideal temperature required to bring a fired piece to *maturity* may prevent it from attaining its full potential beauty. Because of the wide variation in glass manufacturing formulas, various glasses expand and contract at different rates when exposed to heat; therefore the separate parts of a laminated glass object should be cut from a single piece of glass, if possible. They should at least be cut from similar glass made by the same manufacturer. Otherwise the fired piece may eventually crack apart due to the differences in expansion of its separate glass components.

Beautiful bent and laminated glass objects can be formed with stained glass, but window glass and stained glass cannot be fused or bent together by heat. Inevitably they crack apart because of the wide difference between their coefficients of expansion. Window glass can be given color with glass ices, glass enamels, overglazes, and metallic lusters developed especially to be compatible with all glass when it is fired. Some different colors of the same type stained glass do not remain fused together without cracking. This is especially likely to occur when reds, oranges, and red golds are fused to other colors of glass, but they may fuse to one another successfully. All glass should be test-fired before a fused project is begun. Metallic oxides, carbonates, and other chemical ingredients added to the glass batch to color it, to lower its melting point, to control viscosity, or to attain a workable temperature range give each glass color, type, and thickness its individual rate of expansion. However, stained glass shapes can be fired separately to round their edges and they can then be bonded together, to double-strength window glass, or to plate glass with an epoxy resin made especially for bonding glass to glass.

Most window glass begins to sag almost imperceptibly at 1100°F and settles into its mold at 1250°–1300°F, depending upon the glass thickness. It reaches the top heat required to round its edges at 1400°–1450°F. Both blanks of glass for a lamination may be fired flat separately to the heat required to round the glass edges and thereafter be combined and positioned on the mold to settle into it together. Or they can be laminated flat together before they are positioned on the mold and sagged. If the glass has not been given this prefiring treatment to round the edges, it is left in the kiln on its mold to complete the firing after it has sagged. Glass that has prefired must fire just long enough to settle completely into the mold. It must be annealed after each firing to assure that it will not split or crack between operations.

Stained glass begins to sag at 1000°F and settles into the mold by 1150°F. The edges become softly rounded by 1300°–1350°F. The color variations in each sheet of antique stained glass are so vibrant they need no other embellishment than the form they take when they are contoured over a mold.

Whenever the top glass for a lamination is decorated with powdered glass colorant on the surface that will be turned over and positioned against the lower glass, it must be given an extra spraying with enameling gum. Otherwise some of the glass ice or enamel is sure to drop off the glass when it is turned over. Hold the glass at arm's length and spray it gently so the spray does not blow off the enamel. Dry it completely before the glass is reversed and lowered onto the bottom sheet of glass. (See Section 5, "Decorating Methods and Projects," for additional information on decorating laminations.)

GLASS BENT BY DRAPING

A small disc mold is positioned on top of a column of insulation brick and a 10-inch glass circle is centered over it and fired for an exciting bent glass project. To make the mold, bend a strip of linoleum, shiny side in, to make a 3½-inch circle; tie a string around it to hold it temporarily. Set it on a section of formica board or a sheet of glass and press a clay coil all around the base to secure it and to prevent the mold mix from running out. Paint the inside of the linoleum and the base with a light oil, such as baby oil or vegetable oil, so the mold will release easily. Consult the directions under "Glass Casting" for making the mold mixture. When the glass bends around the disc mold in the heat of the kiln, it may prevent the disc from being removed easily. To facilitate removal, implant a flat coil of nichrome wire into the small mold circle before the mixture sets. After the glass is bent and cooled, a firm tug on the wire will crumble the expendable mold and make it easy to remove.

When the glass is positioned on its "pedestal" mold and set into a cool kiln, follow regular firing procedures. The glass will begin to bend down in an arc at 1200°F. Watch it closely through the peephole. At about 1300°F, it will form gentle curves around the edge. The kiln is shut off and vented. It is important to avoid opening the door unnecessarily or too often because this will lower the temperature near the door and slow the bending in that area. Gold or silver luster or painted designs can be applied to the glass before it is bent or for a second firing. Fire the luster to 1000°F if the glass has already been bent.

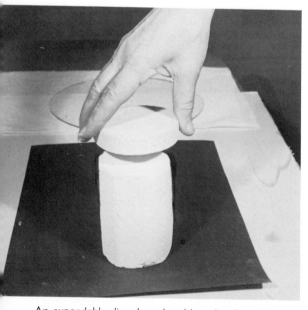

An expendable disc shaped mold made of equal parts of plaster and Plicast Verilite is positioned on top of a column of insulation brick cut with a hacksaw. The disc and the column were rubbed with kiln wash.

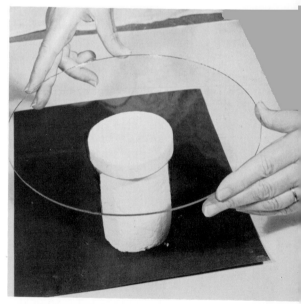

A 10" circle of double-strength window glass is centered over the disc mold. Gold luster can be brushed on the very edge of the glass circle for decorative effect. When the luster dries, the assemblage is transported to the kiln and set back from the door in a front-loading kiln.

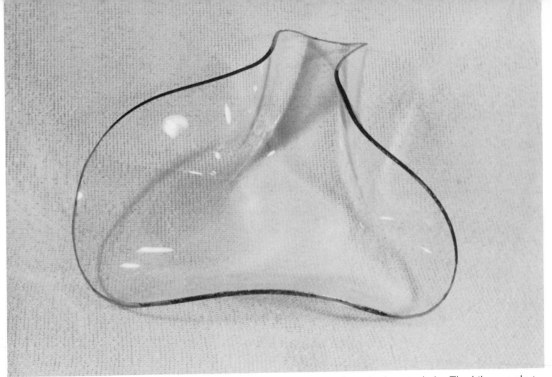

The glass begins to arc at 1200°F. It must be watched closely through the peephole. The kiln was shut off and vented for a few moments at 1300°F. The completed glass form has a gold luster edge.

A small circle of light blue cathedral glass bent further at 1250°F. Stained glass softens at lower temperature than window glass.

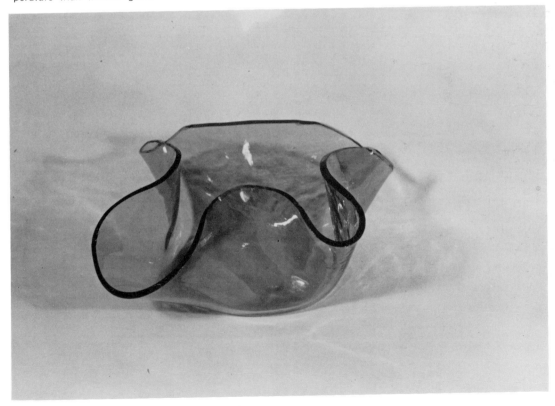

BUBBLES IN LAMINATED GLASS

The bubbles that frequently appear in laminated glass are an accepted and usually beautiful characteristic of fused glass, although large bubbles caused by incorrect firing may not be decorative. Bubbles form in laminations when air spaces are enclosed by powdered glass colorants or any materials that do not leave escape routes for trapped air to travel to the edge of the laminated glass as it fuses. If a bowl has steep sides, bubbles may be entrapped at the point where the base meets the sides of the mold. Included material may continue to hold the glass elevated for a while after the surrounding glass starts to fuse;

small bubbles clustered around the inclusion can be exciting.

Bubbles are induced in a lamination if you add tiny dots of fresh baking soda to the lower glass wherever you want them. A general bubble effect is achieved if a pinch of baking soda is blended in some powdered colorant and sifted over the lower glass. Whenever an even layer of powdered glass color is sifted over the glass in a lamination, to avoid unwanted bubbles, sift a little extra layer of the powder or colorless glass flux in the center area; the centers will fuse first and force air to the outside edge where it can escape.

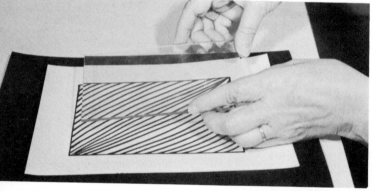

A square of single-strength window glass is laid over a design of freehand drawn lines.

Small squares of thick cardboard are taped against each side of the glass to hold it in place. A wood "bridge" supports the hand to steady it while lines of squeegee oil are traced over the drawn lines.

Dark enamel is sifted generously over the drawn lines.

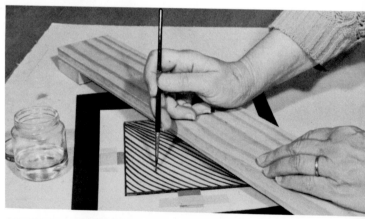

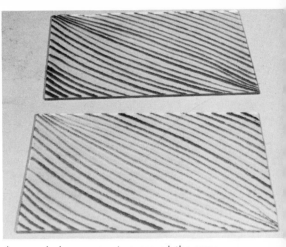

Excess enamel is tapped from the glass.

A second glass square is prepared the same way. The glass must be "baked" on aluminum foil in a warm oven at 350°F to drive off gases from the oil before it is fused.

One glass square is turned over and lowered carefully onto the other glass. They are fired to 1450°F to fuse the glass.

The casually drawn lines make a varied and interesting pattern of bubbles.

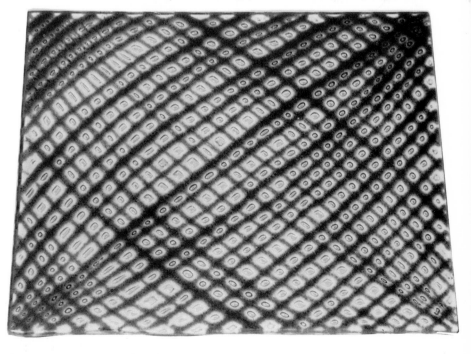

Laminated plate. Glenda Davis. The two circles of glass were enameled and sprayed with enameling gum. Lines were scratched through the powder on each circle and the two were laminated for this attractive effect.

Light transparent enamel is sifted all over the glass. A tiny sifter dusts red opaque enamel in a trailed design.

A pointed wooden skewer scratches holes in the red design.

A second clear glass circle is positioned over the enamel-covered glass.

The two are lowered carefully and exactly centered on the prepared mold, which has been sifted with fresh kiln wash.

The glass has slumped and edges are fused at 1450°F.

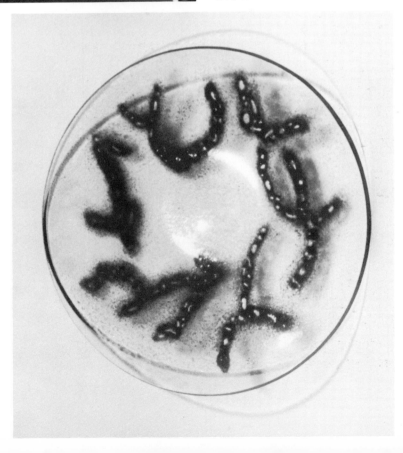

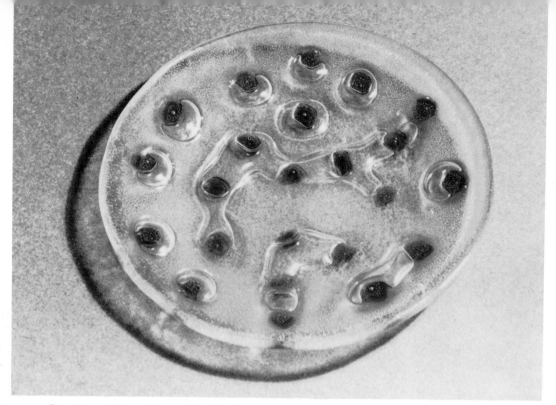

Fused tray. Alden Abbott. Two 7'' glass circles with small squares of colored bottle glass laminated between them and slumped.

Two glass circles laminated. Alden Abbott. Lines were drawn through enamels in a gentle arc on each circle of glass. They were sprayed with enameling gum and dried, then fused together.

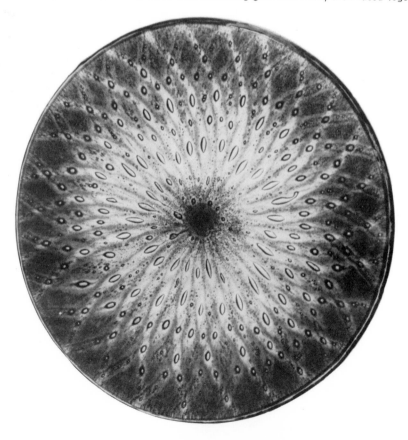

PREFORMED GLASS OBJECTS

Discarded glass bottles have endless possibilities as potential decorative objects; fired rings cut from bottles make wonderful units in mosaics or for jewelry. Most commercial bottles are made of "soft" glass that is low fusing. Since many of them are very thick however, especially wine bottles, they must often be fired as high as 1550°F to 1600°F to fuse them flat. The glass fires to a lovely silken gloss that gives them great depth of color. The bottom of a bottle is very bulky and can be massive when it folds or collapses toward the top of the bottle, which it always does in firing flat. It is advisable to remove this unwieldly section of glass before the bottle is slumped into a mold. A round bottle that is laid horizontal in its mold tends to roll sideways. To prevent it from rolling, sift an extra amount of kiln wash at the point of contact, then sink the bottle on it. This should hold it.

Bottle cutting should be practiced on any available ordinary bottles before you risk an especially attractive specimen. It requires considerable practice to make a clean severance. Although theoretically bottles can be scored and separated by adhering masking tape around the bottle, then scoring an unbroken line along the tape with a glass cutter, when you start to score, the cutter tends to skitter off on a path of its own choice as you press it against the slick curved glass. There are several excellent types of bottle cutters on the market and they are accompanied by detailed instructions and suggestions for their use. The one in the demonstration project can be used to cut various sizes of glass bottles and jugs; and it costs only a few dollars. Investing in one of these gadgets is more rewarding than trying to improvise a cutter.

For the illustrated project, the bottom and threaded top of the green wine bottle were removed. A slab clay mold was made to follow the contours of the bottle but leaving extra inches to allow for the glass stretching

Wall hanging. BoBo Zinn. All segments of glass are laminated with enamels sgraffitoed and bubbles achieved with seven parts enamel mixed with one part baking soda. *Photo by Drew Henery.*

out as the bottle flattened. Coils of clay were laid under the edges of the slab to give it a shallow contour as the clay dried. It was fired slowly to cone 08 (or 1800°F). Then the kiln was turned off and left to cool completely before the mold was removed.

The wine bottle was fired to 1600°F to flatten it as it slumped into the mold. It was annealed for two hours because of the thickness of the glass. When the bottle tray cooled, long stripes of gold metallic luster were brushed from one end to the other on the tray. The luster was fired to 1000°F.

Almost any kind of bottle or jar can be made attractive when it is mosaicked with very small glass tesserae. Flat-sided bottles or flasks are easy to decorate, but curved ones require a little patience. Because it takes some time for epoxy to set, only one row can be affixed at a time on a curved surface. Additional glass would slide off before it adhered. On this kind of surface, the glass pieces should be narrow. A round jar or bottle is laid horizontal and anchored between two sticks that are tacked to a board. Epoxy the tesserae and apply a row along the ridge of the horizontal plane and let it set before you begin the next row. Be sure to use special glass adhesive. When the board and bottle are set up in a convenient out-of-the-way place, the rows can be applied while other activities are going on. If the epoxy is mixed correctly (and the room temperature is not below 70°F), it should set firm in three hours. Three or four rows can be applied in one day. For additional instruction on mosaics, see "Mosaics" in Section 3.

The left hand swings the cutter toward the right hand, which holds the bottle firm at the top. The bottle is rotated clockwise as the left hand continues to score it with the cutter.

A tapper that comes with the cutter taps under the score line. As soon as a crack appears, the glass is tapped just ahead of the crack on the scored line until the crack has developed all around the bottle. The glass should separate with a final sharp rap of the tapper.

The prepared clay slab mold is sifted with kiln wash before the bottle is positioned. The bottle's top and bottom have been removed.

The fired bottle tray is decorated with long stripes of gold luster. The shape of the mold has given the narrow end a gentle curve.

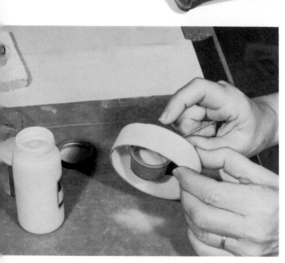

To give color to glass rings cut from colorless bottles, spray them with enameling gum and sift high-fire transparent or opaque glass ices or enamels over inside and outside of a ring before it is fired flat.

A colorless small bottle ring was given coats of imperial blue and light turquoise transparent enamels, then it was fused flat. Fused glass jewels made from scraps of colored glass were epoxied to the ring and to one another only at *points of contact*. The open spaces between them give a delicate effect. (For making the little glass "Jewels," see Section 6.)

A round lidded candy jar is laid horizontal and anchored between two sticks tacked to a board. Stained glass tesserae are epoxied along the ridge of the horizontal plane. The epoxy must set before the next row of glass is applied.

Grout is applied with a very flexible rubber spatula.

The completed mosaicked candy jar. Notice that a few additional glass pieces were cemented on top of the glass in several places to give a more sculptural effect.

RECYCLE YOUR BOTTLES INTO "STAINED GLASS"

The countless methods and objects that are made from emptied bottles alone comprise a fascinating glasscraft. Glass artist Bruce Laughlin, known for his beautiful fused and bent glass, suggests a way to recycle colored and clear glass bottles by making "stained glass" for use in leaded, bonded, or bent work. The clear glass is colored with sifted glass ices and enamels after it is flattened.

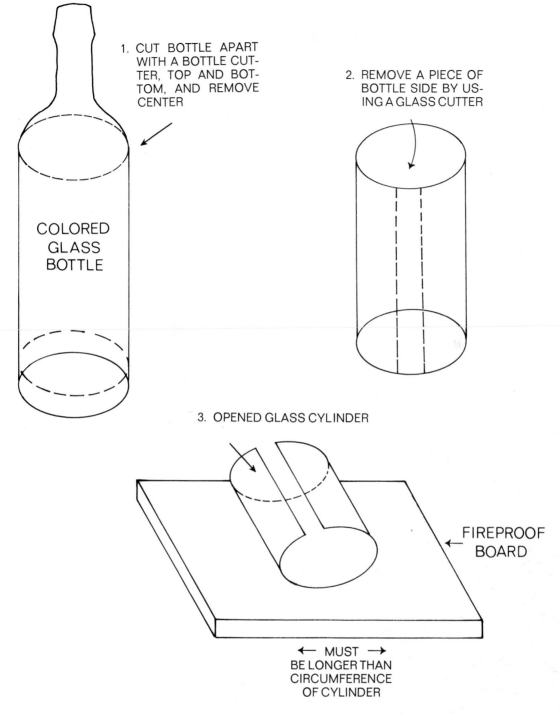

1. CUT BOTTLE APART WITH A BOTTLE CUTTER, TOP AND BOTTOM, AND REMOVE CENTER

COLORED GLASS BOTTLE

2. REMOVE A PIECE OF BOTTLE SIDE BY USING A GLASS CUTTER

3. OPENED GLASS CYLINDER

FIREPROOF BOARD

← MUST →
BE LONGER THAN CIRCUMFERENCE OF CYLINDER

Bruce Laughlin's make-your-own stained glass idea. A section of bottle is cut open and fired flat. The small colored glass rectangles can be used for leaded or bonded glass. If the narrow strip is not removed from the glass before it is fired flat, the glass will fuse shut again instead of opening out flat in the kiln heat. The glass should flatten at 1200°F. It is annealed for two hours if it is thicker than ⅛".

Mold-blown jar, designed, sandblasted, and etched by Polly Rothenberg.

5
Decorating Methods and Projects

DECORATING LAMINATIONS

THE objective in laminating two or more layers of glass is to entrap materials that will give decorative effects between the layers that could not be fired to the top surface of the glass. For example, the enamels fired to metal are not always compatible with glass, but they can be fired between glass layers if they are not applied too thickly. Other materials such as flattened silver wire, underglazes, stenciled patterns in glass ices and enamels, very fine glass crushings, enamel threads, and combinations of these materials can be laminated safely.

Laminated materials must be thin, flat, and dispersed over the surface of the lower glass so bare glass spaces are left between them. The bare spaces fuse to the covering glass and seal the lamination together. Small bubbles form around these entrapped designs and add to the decorative effect. Both sheets of glass must be clean and of identical glass. Small dabs of Elmer's Glue-all will hold the material to the glass and should keep them in place until they can be safely positioned in the kiln. The materials to be laminated must be completely dry before you combine both sheets of glass on the mold, ready for firing.

COLORANTS FOR BENT AND LAMINATED GLASS

Special glass ices, enamels, and painting colors are formulated with the correct coefficient of expansion to fit glass that will be fired. Glass ices are available in *high-fire* and *low-fire* colors designated as HF and LF. The high-fire ice colors are fired on the surface and between flat or contoured laminated glass by firing them to 1500°F–1600°F. The glass must be annealed after the colors are fired on it. Low-fire colors will fuse to the surface of glass objects at about 1050°F–1100°F. These low-fire colors are useful for decorating glass that will not be bent or laminated. Each series includes a clear glass flux that is sifted lightly over glass surfaces to assure a sparkling finish and subtle texturing. A small amount of regular metal enamels can be used *in combination* with high-fire glass ices for laminations where additional or intensified colors are wanted. Most metal enamels are generally unsatisfactory when they are used alone on glass surfaces, but they can be laminated between two glass sheets if they are not applied too thick. In combination with glass ices, a ratio of four parts glass ice to one part metal enamel is suggested.

The glass ices and enamels used for

projects in this book are 80-mesh powders. To apply them to glass, a thin layer of adhesive such as light oil or enameling gum is applied to the glass surface before the glass colors are sifted in a thin layer with an 80-mesh sifter. When the glass has been cleaned thoroughly with a thin solution of detergent water, brush it with squeegee oil or lavender oil. Or agar, Klyrfire, or other enameling gum can be applied with a power sprayer or aerosol spray unit in a solution thinned with water so it will go through the sprayer. Spray guns or atomizers manipulated by hand may give erratic distribution of the spray that makes droplets or other disfigurations in the enamel layer. Once the two glasses are laminated, these unwanted marks cannot be eliminated. Dry the glass thoroughly before it is fired. Oils must be baked off at 300°F before the glass is laminated.

Decorating colors for *painting on glass* are easily mixed with one of several mediums, depending on the decorating problem. The powdered kind should be mixed with squeegee oil or other light painting oil where slow drying is desirable. The powders should be mixed with water, Klyrfire, or other enameling gum for painting, spot decoration, or laminated color. The decorating colors are bought in *low fire* (1100°F) and *high fire* (1500°F). The low-fire series are used either for glass surfaces where no distortion is planned or where bending has already taken place. The high-fire series are used for surface decoration of glass that will be slumped or laminated. Moisture or oils must be driven off by slow drying in a warm place before colorants are laminated between glass layers. Otherwise the fumes may be trapped and may discolor the glass. *Ready-mixed moist colors* are applied with a fine pointed brush.

Glass ices, enamels, and dry and moist painting colors used in projects in this book were from Thomas C. Thompson Company. Other companies that sell glass colorants are listed in Supply Sources. Eighty-mesh sifters with convenient handles are available at metal enamel supply stores.

Glass bowl. R. Bruce Laughlin. Enamels and glass ices are laminated between two glass circles and slumped in a mold. Lines were sgraffitoed through a design for this stunning effect.

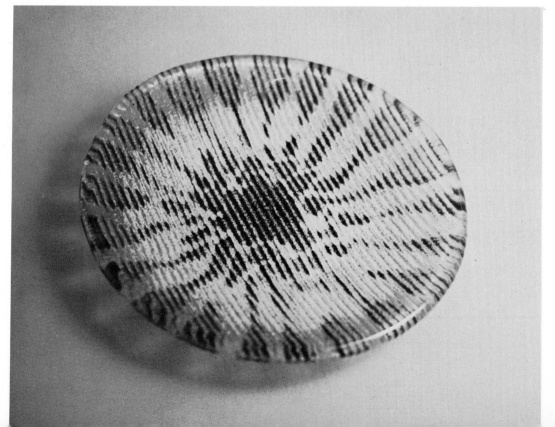

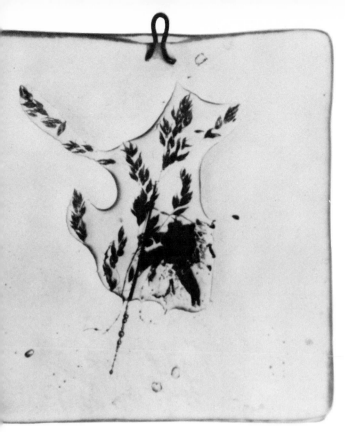

Laminated glass panel. Glenda Davis. Weeds fused between two panels of window glass become black and charred but retain their forms. The gray area is smoked glass resulting from the fumes of the weeds as they were heated.

Ragweed fused in glass. Glenda Davis.

Weed fused in glass. Glenda Davis.

EMBOSSED GLASS

When small glass shapes are fired to a glass base, all the applied pieces and the base must be cut from one variety of glass made by the same manufacturer. Clean all the glass with detergent water, rinse it well and dry it. Dabs of Elmer's Glue-all will hold the small pieces in position until they are fused. Colored glass decorating powders are sifted over them either before or after they are positioned, depending upon the desired effect. Fire the assemblage until the edges of the applied glass and the base are rounded, about 1350°F for window glass. Although stained glass cannot be fired successfully to window glass, a beautiful effect can be achieved when stained glass shapes are fired flat separately to round their edges and are subsequently epoxied to the window glass base.

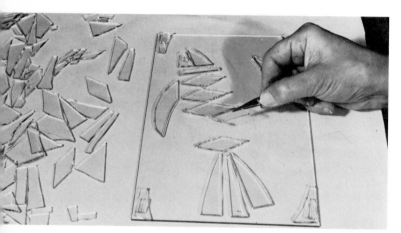

GLASS SEASCAPE

Clear glass fragments are tentatively positioned on a rectangle to develop a design.

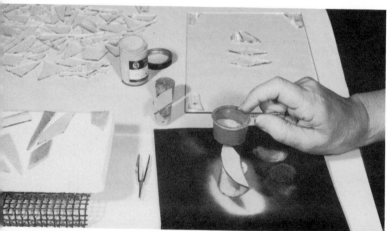

Individual pieces are sifted with low-firing powdered glass colors and placed on a slice of prepared insulation brick to fire the colors.

All the glass pieces are stuck to the glass panel with dabs of Elmer's Glue-all to keep them from shifting before they are fired.

Siftings of blue, green, and aqua transparent glass ices are applied to the background and glass "seaweeds." It does not matter if some of the color drifts onto the fish design.

A kiln shelf has been prepared with a light sifting of kiln wash as a separator. The glass panel is lowered carefully onto the shelf. The glue holds everything secure. It will fire out in the kiln and leave no ash.

Glass seascape in blue, aqua, turquoise, and purple.

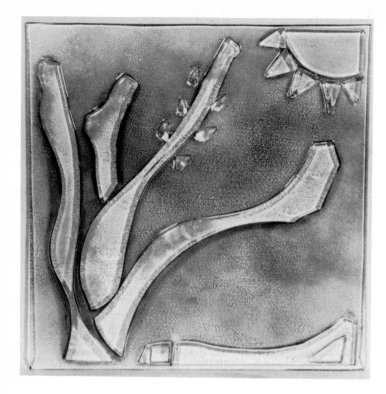

Glass landscape. The embossed shapes are glued in place with bits of Elmer's glue before glass ices are sifted over them. Chartreuse is sifted on the applied shapes and transparent red over the background with the colors merging. The panel is given one firing to 1350°F.

THE SAILBOAT. Glenda Davis. Transparent and opaque blues, transparent green, opaque orange, and white.

Fused panel. BoBo Zinn. A wedge of glass with added smaller pieces of glass is covered with a combination of blue and green glass ices and opaque enamels. It is fired until it is glowing red and molten on the kiln shelf. Edges are pulled up and pleated with a firing tool while the glass is still in the kiln. (Gloves must be worn for this method.) A clear glass panel is fired without color to achieve rounded edges and attach the hook. The two panels are bonded with R-TV Glue. Overall size: 10" X 4". *Photo by Drew Henery.*

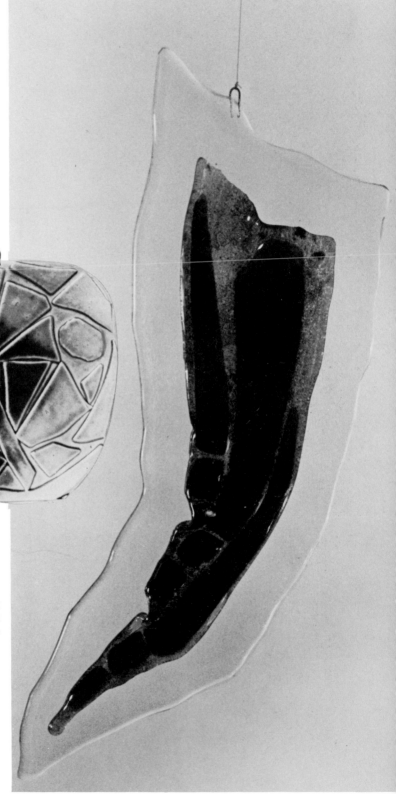

FISH. Glenda Davis. Lamination in planned fragmentation. Center is in opaque blues, outside area in transparent blues.

BOTTLES. Glenda Davis. Fused fragments. Transparent colors in green, blue, pink, and tan.

3D Form. Alden Abbott. Small single-strength triangles are fused flat on the circle. Extra-thick triangles are fused on edge.

Brown stained glass geese heads were fired to round their edges. They are traced on paper to locate their position for a panel design.

The panel was prepared with stenciled heads of flying geese and corner hangers fired on it. The stained glass shapes are epoxied to the background glass.

FLIGHT OF THE BROWN GEESE. The thin strips of clear glass epoxied over stenciled heads of flying geese are drifting clouds. Colorless glass waves epoxied over the brown geese are a third layer of bonded glass. Part of an orange moon is bonded to the upper right corner. This is an example of both fused and bonded glass to develop an idea.

PAINTING ON STAINED GLASS— FIRED

The lavish painting of stained glass cathedral windows during the final stages of the Renaissance cast the art into controversy for centuries, but today the restrained and thoughtful use of fired paints can add variation and emphasis to stained glass designs. In leaded glass, the leads form the chief linear expression. Glass paint should not interfere with the integrity of the lead line design nor obscure the pervasive beauty of transparent stained glass.

This demonstration project does not include leads. Small squares of green gold antique glass depend on the black painted lines for decorative design. Although the complex professional painting applied to large windows requires methods and skills beyond the simple treatment described here, linear patterns and judicious brushstrokes applied with glass paint are another of the many techniques well within the ability of the serious amateur.

Prepare glass in the usual way by washing it with a thin solution of detergent water. Rinse it with warm water and dry it. Tape it over a design drawn on paper that extends beyond the glass. The square of glass and the pattern taped to the underside of it are rotated together on the light box as the work progresses. Apply your brushstrokes in the direction that is easiest for you to control, by simply turning the paper. An armrest or "bridge," made from a board with flat wood blocks nailed under each end, will elevate your hand and wrist above the glass surface while you work. It will prevent them from smearing the paint or soiling the glass with oil from your skin, which can cause the paint to "skip." It is advisable to make the bridge long enough that the blocks rest on the frame of the light box rather than on its glass top where undue pressure could crack the glass.

The paint employed in this project is one of Thompson's glass colors. It should fire smooth, shiny, and permanent at 1100°F. These dry powdered paints can be mixed with oil or water-based binders. Lavender oil or squeegee oil do not leave an ash when they are fired. If you prefer a water-based binder, try an agar solution in the proportion of one part liquid agar to three parts water. A commercial medium called Klyrfire can also be used effectively for mixing glass paints. Water-based binders dry rapidly. Oils dry more slowly and should be dried with some mild heat such as 300°F in an oven or on top of a warm kiln. Oil promotes a smooth-flowing application of the paint that does not dry it out on the palette while you are using it. Whether you use water or oil is a matter of personal preference. Several manufacturers make and sell glass paints and binders.

Liner brushes (pure red sable) are excellent for painting fine, long, smooth lines and details. The brush used for this project is a #4 red sable liner. Its bristles are long, thin, and flexible. To mix the paint, heap a small mound of dry powdered glass paint on the palette and add a few drops of paint medium as you blend it with a small palette knife. Work it into a smooth homogeneous mix of good brushing consistency. To load the brush, roll it into the paint to work plenty of pigment into the bristles; then stroke the brush lightly two or three times on the bare glass palette to relieve it of excess paint. It must retain enough paint to flow smoothly through a complete stroke without suddenly going dry. Movement of the brush is controlled with the fingers rather than with the arm or wrist as in oil painting. Rest the palm of your hand on the bridge and make the strokes without too much pressure. Vary the width of lines by rolling the brush as you stroke it. Let the paint dry before you carve away irregularities with a pointed round toothpick, a sliver of pointed bamboo or other scriber.

The paint must dry completely before it is fired. If you are firing only one or two glass pieces, set them on a prepared section of insulation brick that has been rubbed with dry whiting to fill its pores, then sift kiln wash over it. If you are firing several pieces or a large glass shape, they can be fired directly on the kiln shelf. It must be prepared in the usual way with a separator to prevent the glass from sticking to the shelf when it is fired. Lower the glass into position and put it into a cool kiln before you turn on the heat. Keep the glass away from the electric elements; if the kiln loads from the front, position the glass away from the door opening. Turn the switch to *low* and leave the kiln door ajar ½ inch to permit glass paint fumes and any remaining moisture to escape. After a half hour, close the door or lid, but leave vents open and turn the heat to *high*. At 950°F close vents; keep a close watch over the temperature rise. Turn off the kiln when the thermostat indicates 1100°F, or when the paint becomes shiny and smooth. Vent the kiln to halt heat rise. After two or three minutes, close the vents again and let the kiln cool normally, making sure to keep it tightly closed so it does not cool too rapidly. When it has cooled, if the fired paint seems too thin, add a second coat and refire the glass.

Painted effects made with brushes, scratching tools, masking tape, rubber cement, stencils, crumpled toweling, and other texturing devices are possibilities for the craftsman who wants to add this dimension to his glass works. It is for the artist himself to decide.

The ends of a wooden "bridge" rest on the light table frame. A design is outlined, not filled in solid, so work can be observed as painting progresses. Paint one coat and fire it; additional coats can be added.

After the first firing, thin areas will be apparent. If a perfectly opaque design is preferred, paint a second coat and fire it again.

Four small gold antique glass windows in a Colonial door are painted in opaque black.

The demonstration of painting small stained glass panes for a Colonial door is quite simple. Although this book does not cover the painting of large stained glass windows as developed in a large studio, a few words should be said about it here. In one method of painting a window, an easel of plate glass is laid over a design and the stained glass shapes are positioned on the plate. Hot beeswax is spooned on junctures and between joints to secure each glass in the relative position it will occupy in the completed window, allowing for an even spacing between segments that will be filled by the leads. This assures that painted details are carried smoothly across the glass. When the wax is hard, the easel may be placed upright and secured in a window where daylight exists. With a variety of brushes, the skillful glass artist applies details to complete a subject already defined by the vibrant glass colors and the leads.*

* Patrick Reyntiens, *The Technique of Stained Glass.* Watson-Guptill Publications, New York.

Fred Conese waxing up stained glass for painting. *Photo by courtesy of Willet Stained Glass Studios.*

A selection of artist's brushes for painting glass. *Photo by courtesy of Willet Stained Glass Studios.*

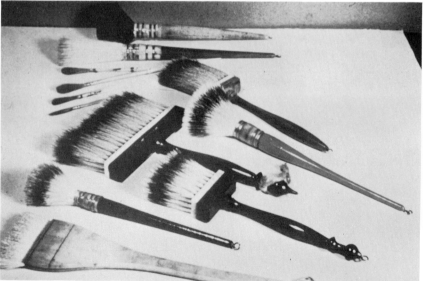

Ray DiHaven painting a waxed-up window with monotone for Willet Stained Glass Studios. The paint is dried and kiln-fired. *Photo by Ted Koepper.*

GLASS PAINTS—UNFIRED

If you prefer to use a glass paint that does not require firing, it is well to select one of the epoxy paints made especially for painting on glass.* The paint usually is sold in large paint stores. At present, it comes in both two-component and ready mixed form in quarts and gallons that are available in several colors. Unless you plan to use all the paint when it is first opened, it is best to select the two-component variety and mix it in the exact proportions indicated on the container.

* Epoxy paint used in the demonstrated project is two-component O'Brien Mira-plate epoxy coating.

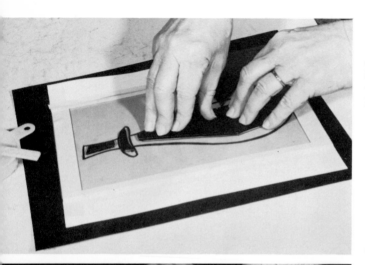

An outline sketch is taped under the glass base. Sections of stained glass are spread with epoxy and pressed firmly in place. Dry it overnight.

Unfired paint with stained glass bonded to clear glass.

A flexible Mack Sword Striper brush #0 with black epoxy paint is traced over the yellow glass, following the bottle sketch underneath it. The light in the table shows up the sketch clearly. Dry the paint for several hours, but do not fire it.

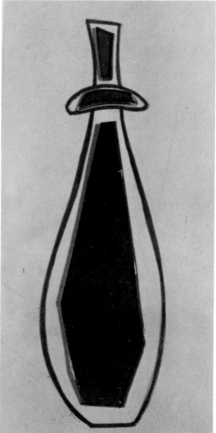

SANDBLASTING AND ENGRAVING

Growing enthusiasm for decorative and functional glass art of all kinds has aroused new interest in surface enrichment of this dramatic transparent material. Increased zeal among craftsmen for etching glass with a sandblaster is prompting large and small colleges to install major sandblasting equipment for use in their regular art programs. Today large art glass studios include sandblasted glass in their commissioned works. Although the equipment represents a substantial investment, especially for the small glass studio, commercial sheet and plate glass companies have begun to offer sandblasting services to their customers. They may etch your properly prepared glass for a fee.

Sandblasting on glass achieves a frosted effect of translucent to transparent contrast. Almost any kind of glass is suitable: sheet crystal, window glass, preformed shapes such as bottles, vases, goblets, and glass sculptures. Stained glass of the "flashed" variety is beau-

tiful when it is etched. Mirrored glass is another favorite for this method. Contemporary artist-craftsmen have a special fondness for etching blown glass sculptures.

To begin, cover the glass all over with masking tape, lapping the strips and making sure the tape is pressed closely against the glass so sand is not forced under it. Be careful to cover all the edges. Draw a simple design on the tape with a sharp pencil point. Using a sharp stencil knife or single-edge razor blade, cut around and peel away sections of the tape to reveal areas to be etched. Now the glass is ready for the sandblaster.

The equipment must include an exhaust fan for drawing off silica dust that is harmful to the lungs. A compressor is required to blast out the stream of special cutting sand. A coarse sand called flint shot, made from St. Peter's sandstone quarried in the Midwest, and carborundum grains are two abrasives commonly used on glass. Heavy gloves sealed

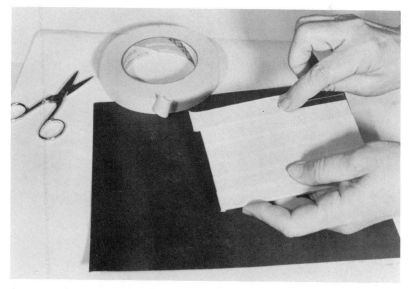

Cover the glass all over with lapped strips of masking tape. Be sure to cover the edges.

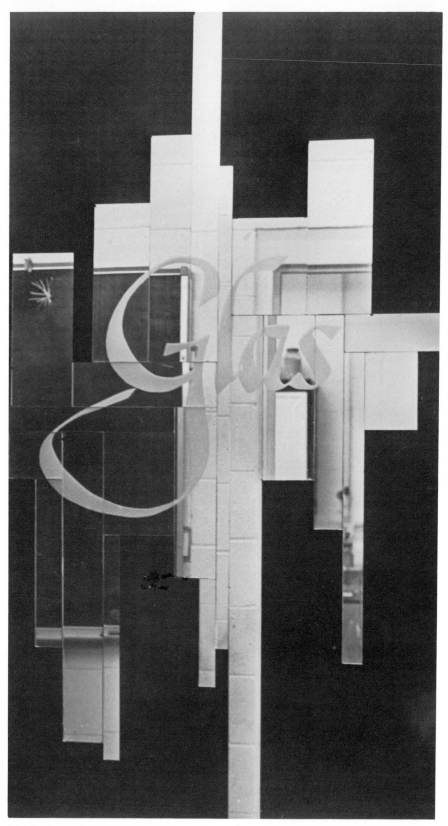

Mural of mirrored glass with designs etched by sandblasting. The Georgian College of Applied Arts and Technology, Barrie, Ontario. *Georgian College photos by Marc Robillard.*

into openings in the front wall of the sand-blasting machine allow you to thrust your hands into the gloves that project into a lighted airtight interior. You can view the interior through a window while you manipulate the glass, constantly turning and revolving it under the forced sand, controlled by a foot switch outside the machine. There are different-sized machines to suit a variety of requirements.

When the frosted glass is removed from the machine, parts of the design can be taken further. If tape is peeled from the glass to reveal clear areas, new tape can be masked over certain sections of the etched and clear glass and it is returned to the sandblaster to achieve deeper or lighter carving and shading. In addition, a combination of sandblasting and engraving can give the glass design an airy lightness.

Linear designs are drawn into the glass surface with an engraving tool. There are many types of engravers; the one described here is a small hand-held electric tool. A dental drill with a variety of tips is excellent for engraving on glass. The artist who is adept with freehand sketching may be able, with practice, to engrave directly and freely. Others will need to tape a pattern to the underside of the glass and engrave over its guiding lines. It is advisable to practice on scraps or small rectangles of glass to work out ideas for strokes before embarking on any glass engraving projects. Fine lines are incised by holding the engraving tool as vertical as possible. For matting broad areas, tilt it on the side and skim or vibrate it lightly over the glass. To engrave deeply, inscribe a succession of light strokes, one over the other. Above all, do not be disheartened by your initial shaky strokes. With practice, you will find that instead of striking small blows that take your tool off on a tangent, you are beginning to achieve firm skillful strokes. Engraving glass will become a delight.

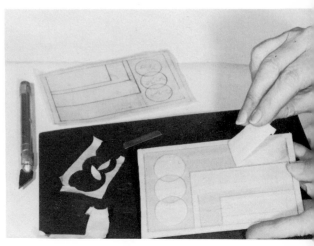

Cut around and peel away certain sections of the tape to reveal the areas of the glass you want to etch.

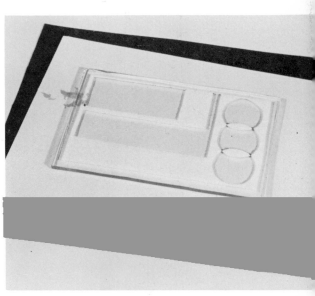

The sandblasted areas cast shadows along their edges, which become part of the design.

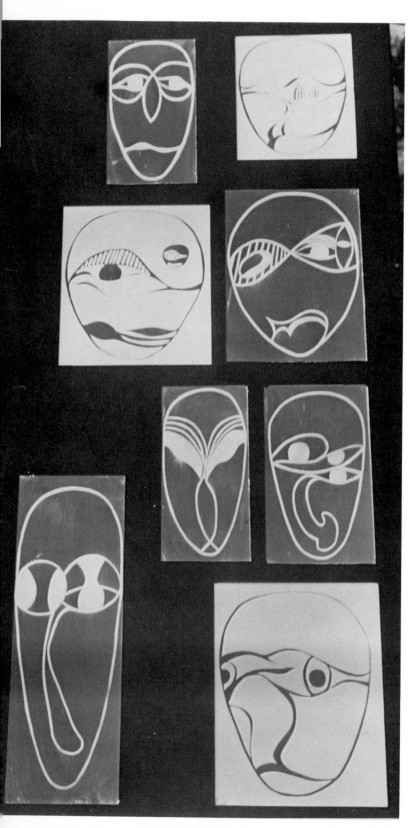

FACES. Glass Design Department of Georgian College. Sandblasting combined with etching on mirrored glass.

▶

Designer Kornelia Meszaros and artist Robin Clarke plan a design for engraving a bowl of blown glass. Glass Design Department, Georgian College.

▶

Engraved strokes are practiced on a glass scrap before the tool is applied to a glass form. To matt broad areas, the tip of the engraver is tilted on its side and skimmed lightly over the glass. Robin Clarke, *left*, and Kornelia Meszaros, *right*.

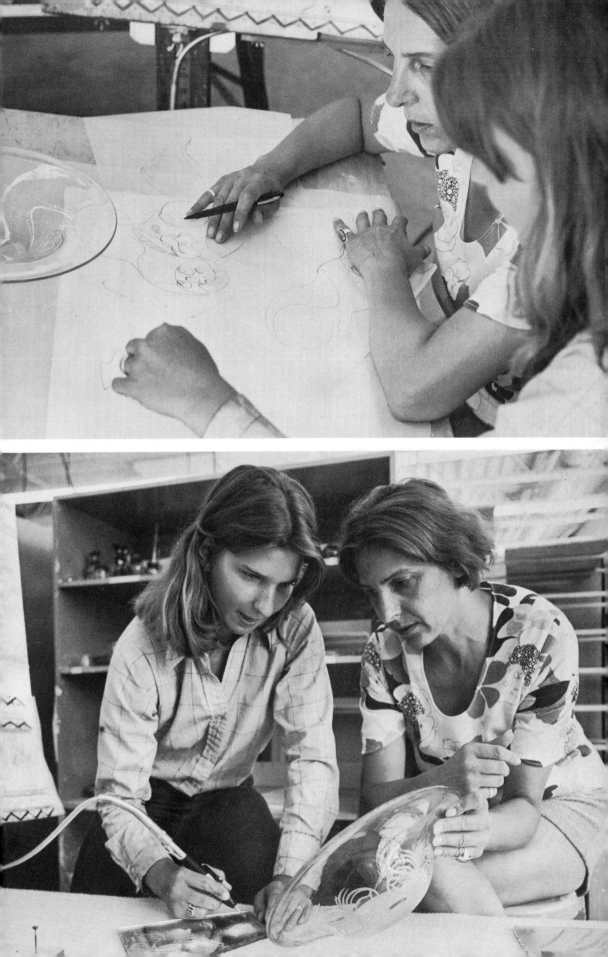

SGRAFFITO

Spray or paint over a glass sheet with enameling gum, then sift colored glass powder over the gum. When it has dried, use any scratching tool to remove lines or spaces in the glass ice or enamel to create a design. The glass can be positioned over a drawn design or you can work it out freehand if you can sketch. A light table is useful if you are using dark powders. In drawing your lines, remember, lines that do not lead off the edge of the glass will likely trap bubbles in the lamination, but not on a top surface. Fired sgraffito lines drawn in light transparent colors are not as pronounced as lines scratched in dark or opaque colors. Metal enamels come in many beautiful and intense colors. They can be used for sgraffito work if they are laminated *between* two glass sheets. If oil is used for the adhesive, it must be baked off in an oven at 350°F before the enamel is sgraffitoed or combined for lamination.

In the demonstrated project, glass rectangles are cut from single-strength window glass. They are washed with detergent water, rinsed and dried. One glass is sprayed with diluted agar solution of one part liquid agar to three parts water, a consistency that will go through a sprayer without clogging it. Deep blue transparent enamels are sifted over the gummed surface and dried. The enamel is sgraffitoed with two combs in a pattern of crossed lines that lead off the glass edges. The enamel is sprayed again with gum and *dried*. A clear glass rectangle is lowered gently onto the prepared glass that has been positioned on a kiln shelf sifted with kiln wash. The combined glass sheets will be fused flat before they are slumped on a clay mold. If you have a steady hand, they can be positioned together on the mold and fired in one operation to slump them.

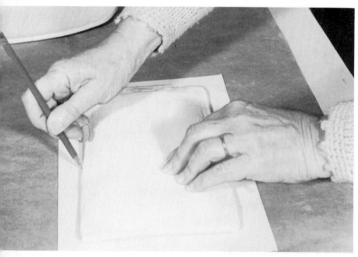

The outline of a mold for a rectangular tray is traced on thin cardboard for a pattern.

Two individual sheets of single-strength window glass are cut around the pattern.

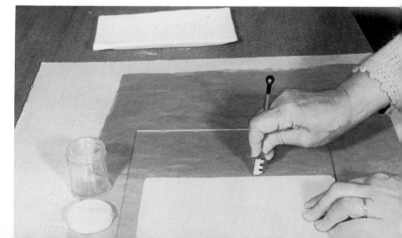

One glass is sprayed with a solution of three parts water to one part agar.

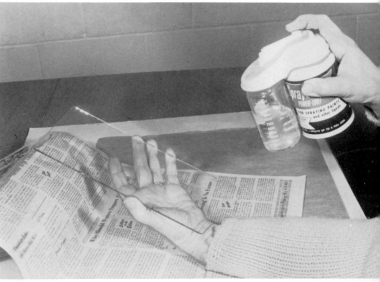

The glass is propped on corks so it can be picked up easily. Transparent blue enamels and glass flux are sifted over it. It is dried and sgraffitoed.

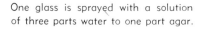

Because regular metal enamels have been used, a second clear glass sheet is laminated to it and fired flat on the kiln shelf. Notice the small combs on the left that were the scratching tools. Firing temperature is 1400°F to blunt edges and fuse the enamels.

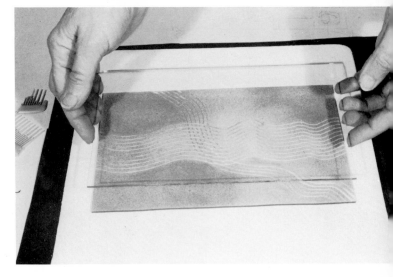

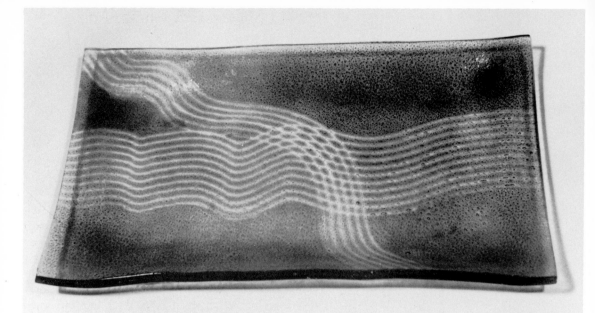

The laminated glass is slumped on a clay mold to 1300°F.

Sgraffitoed glass panel. Alden Abbott.

LAMINATED SILVER FOIL AND STENCIL

To laminate powdered glass colorants or other materials between two layers of glass that will be decorated and slumped, preparatory processes are planned in a workable sequence. In the demonstrated project employing silver foil and stenciled glass enamels, the silver foil areas are applied and fired first.

Clean the glass and dry it. Position the bottom glass layer over a drawn design. The design area that will become foil is transferred to tracing paper. Place a foil sheet between the traced design and another sheet of tracing paper. Cut out the design through the two sheets of tracing paper and the silver foil. The foil is too fragile to be cut by itself. With the foil still held between the tracing paper, lay it on a firm surface and prick holes all over it with a sharp needle. These holes will permit gases and moisture to escape as the foil is fired.

Brush enameling gum on the planned foil location on the glass; immediately press a damp brush on the foil cutout and transfer it to the gummed area on the flat glass. A long piece of foil should be cut and applied in sections. Smooth it out with the brush, stroking it from center to edge to work out excess gum and smooth away wrinkles. After you have dried it in a warm place for at least an hour, insert the glass into a cool kiln and follow regular glass firing procedures to 1350°–1400°F. When the glass is annealed and cooled, mask off the glass on each side of the silver foil with pieces of firm paper towel (the kind in commercial paper towel dispensers, not the soft stretchy kind), spray it with enameling gum, and sift transparent glass ice or enamel over the silver. In the project illustrated, paper towel strips also mask off the glass around the center rectangular area, and light green transparent enamel is sifted over the center. When the stencil is removed, the glass is set aside while the second glass is prepared.

Because the two glass sheets must *register* or match their designs, it is important to reverse the design on the second glass, which will be placed upside down over the first glass with their enameled sides together for firing and fusing them. Trace the design on regular translucent tracing paper with a fine-pointed felt tipped marker so it is easily seen when you turn it upside down under the second glass as a guide for decorating it. The second glass is also reversed because it is a free-form design and must register with the shape of the lower glass when they are positioned one over the other. Place the second glass over the reversed design.

String is the stencil for a linear design that appears as a sgraffitoed pattern in the completed tray. To give the string some body and make it manageable, it is soaked with enameling gum. Then it is laid out on the glass following the drawn lines on the design under the glass. A stencil of firm paper toweling blocks off the rectangular area in the center while enameling gum is sprayed over the glass, the strings, and the paper stencil. Green transparent enamel is sifted quickly over all before the adhesive gum dries out. When the paper stencil and the strings have been removed, spray the enamel again, holding the enameled glass at arm's length from the sprayer so the enamel already applied does not blow off the glass. An adequate amount of adhesive will ensure that the enamel does not fall off when the glass is reversed over the lower glass section. Set the prepared piece aside to dry.

It is advisable to assemble the glass sheets near the kiln to avoid the hazard of disturbing the work enroute to the kiln. Place the lower glass on its mold before you reverse the top glass and gently lower it into position. It must be perfectly registered at the moment it touches the enamel surface below it. Fire the lamination to 1450°F so the edges are firmly combined and rounded. Anneal it for at least an hour as it cools because of the thickness of two laminated glass layers. Gold luster accents are applied and fired to 1000°F. The tray is annealed as it cools.

Smooth out the foil with a damp brush, stroking it to work out wrinkles. It is dried and fired to 1350° F.

Mask off the glass on each side of the foil with paper toweling stencils, then spray it with gum and sift transparent glass enamel over the silver foil.

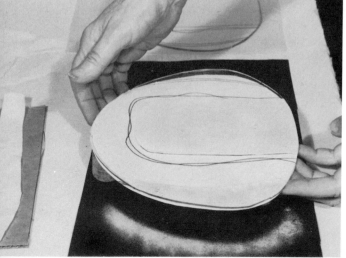

Enamel is sifted over the center area; when the stencils are removed, the glass is set aside while the second glass is prepared.

String is the stencil for a linear design that appears as a sgraffitoed pattern in the composition. Or the lines may be sgraffitoed with a pointed tool after the enamel is sifted.

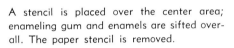

A stencil is placed over the center area; enameling gum and enamels are sifted over-all. The paper stencil is removed.

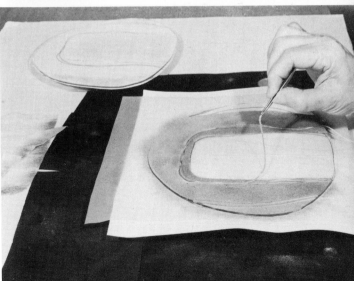

The string stencils are picked off with tweezers.

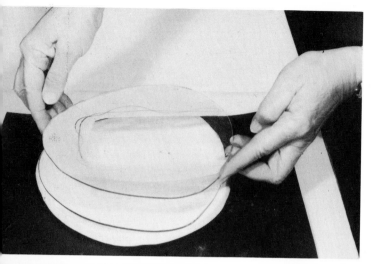

Place the lower glass on its mold before you reverse the top glass and gently lower it into position. Be sure it is registered perfectly before it touches the enamel surface beneath it. The glass is laminated and slumped at 1400°F.

The design is emphasized with gold luster lines applied with a #4 sable liner. A wooden "bridge" steadies the hand with the brush. When the luster dries it is fired to 1000°F.

The completed tray.

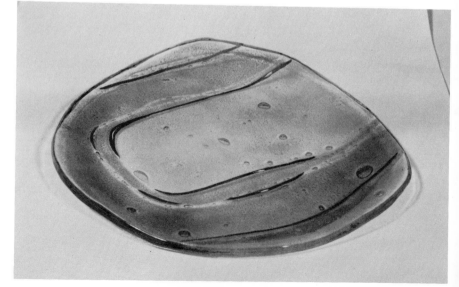

METALLIC LUSTERS

Liquid gold and platinum metallic overglazes (lusters) add glamor to fired surfaces when they are applied with restraint. Clean the glass with detergent water, rinse it well and dry it. Use a good-quality thin flexible brush such as a china painting tracer or liner or a small Oriental watercolor brush. A brush of poor quality may shed hairs on the luster and spoil the finish when the hairs burn out. Luster essence should be bought when the luster is purchased. Only a drop or two is required to keep the metallic paint flowing smoothly. The lusters are applied and fired as the final touch to a completed bent or fused piece. During the application, if any luster is smeared on the glass, remove it at once with alcohol, wiping it off two or three times. Let the piece dry in a warm place for several hours before you fire it.

Position the glass in a cool kiln and turn the switches to *low*. Leave the door partly open for at least ½ hour to slowly drive off fumes from the luster oils. Then continue with regular firing procedures until the temperature reaches 1000°F. Follow the regular cooling and annealing schedule.

Sculptured necklace. Beth and Larry Beede. Constructed of single-strength window glass colored with glass powders in black, brown shading to orange, and clear glass combined with stencils. Nichrome wire loops are fused in place with tabs of glass. Braided strands of leather, handmade beads, and black feathers complete the composition. *Photo by Erik Redlich.*

6
Glass Jewelry

THE methods and materials that can be combined with glass to make delightful jewelry are endless. Small glass jewelry shapes with laminated silver wire or nichrome wire hangers have great versatility as units for constructing all sorts of objects such as bracelets, bolos, pendants, necklaces, and other articles of personal adornment. Use either stained glass or single-strength window glass colored by firing glass decorating powders over the shapes after they have been cut.

All the techniques discussed so far can be adapted in miniature to making jewelry. Contoured or bent glass, laminated fine silver wire designs, alone or in combination with other materials, crushed glass fused to glass and also combined with enameled copper, melted glass jewels, glossy glass chunks tumbled in a lapidary tumbler and combined with wire, hammered metal, leather and feathers, are some of the possibilities explored here. As you work with these materials, you will discover other additional methods of making imaginative jewelry for yourself and for others.

CONTOURED GLASS PENDANTS

To make clay molds for the glass shapes, model white ungrogged sculpture clay (cone 06) so the top surface of each mold contour is broadly shallow and the bottom is flat and level. Avoid undercuts that will prevent the release of glass pieces when they have sagged into the molds. Carve a tiny channel through the *top* of the side wall on each mold to allow air to escape when the hot glass slumps into the mold cavity. If this is neglected, when the glass is fired a large unwanted trapped air bubble may rise under the sagging glass and distort it. Dry and fire the clay molds to cone 06. When they have cooled, paint their tops with whiting (calcium carbonate) dissolved in water to thin cream consistency. Then sift dry kiln wash lightly over the top of the mold. Let the molds dry completely before they are used. Kiln wash should be brushed off and fresh siftings added before each time the molds are used. When they are completed, it is time to prepare the glass.

Some glass pendant shapes are cut to match the top perimeter outlines of the small molds. Wash them in detergent water and dry them. If you are using window glass, apply a light film of adhesive oil or enameling gum and sift colored glass powder over each shape before you fire it. Before the glass is positioned on its matching mold, place each mold on a nichrome mesh firing rack (the kind used for enameling); it will facilitate setting them into the kiln and removing them after they are fired and cooled. It is practical to assemble the pendants on a table near the kiln to avoid the hazard of having pieces slide to the floor when they are transported.

A lightweight hanger for each glass unit is made of silver or nichrome wire, 18–20 gauge, bent double and shaped with its ends curled decoratively and flattened. Position it on one end of the glass shape with the bent loop end extending beyond the glass. The wire should not be flattened at the point where it extends beyond the end of the glass; it may weaken and break. A dab of glue will hold it until it is in the kiln. Lay a very small piece of glass over the wire where it rests on the glass unit, but not covering the loop extension. This wire hanger and small glass piece will fuse onto the glass jewelry shape when they are fired together. When everything is in place, check once more to see that the small hangers are still in position and extending beyond the glass edge.

Set the firing rack with its assembled pieces into the cool kiln, which has not yet been turned on. Position it well toward the rear in a front loading kiln or near the center of the shelf in a top loader. Turn the switch to *low* for at least a half hour with the door or lid open about one-half inch to dry out the kiln as the glass warms gradually. Then close the door but leave vents open and turn switches to *high*. Close vents at 950°F. When the temperature reaches 1250°F, check visually to see whether the little pendant shapes are settling into their molds. Stained glass will slump earlier than window glass. As soon as the glass has settled into the molds, turn off

the kiln and open vents for two or three minutes to halt the heat rise. Then close vents and let the kiln cool. The glass is decorated with gold luster or black overglaze and re-fired to 1000°F.

A solution of kiln wash is brushed over small clay molds.

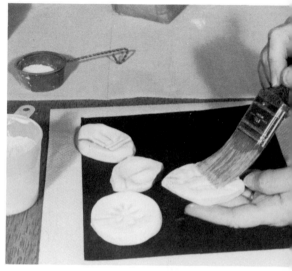

Glass-fluxed pendant shapes are positioned on the clay molds. Notice the wire hangers with tiny glass tabs over them on one end of each pendant form.

The glass is removed from the kiln with a handy firing fork. Each glass has settled into its small mold.

The contoured pendants are decorated with Liquid Gold luster. Dry the gold in a warm spot. Fire it to 1000°F.

The completed pendants.

GLASS AND WOOD JEWELRY

Glass combines attractively with other materials. The illustrated bracelet is formed of yellow stained glass and wire links with polished rosewood units. Cut small rectangles of stained glass, twice as many as the required number of glass links. Sift colorless glass flux on half the links and position them on sections of prepared insulation brick. On top of each of these glass rectangles, position a fine silver or nichrome wire that is long enough that you can bend a loop in each end and also curve the wire decoratively through the glass rectangles that make up each link. If you gently flatten the wires they will stay in place more readily. But do not flatten them where they extend beyond the glass or they will thin too much and will surely break at that point.

Cover each wire on its glass rectangle with one of the remaining small glass rectangles. To hold the top glass pieces in place, dab a bit of Elmer's Glue-all to their underneath surfaces before you position them over the wires. Set the brick support with its glass and wire assemblages on a mesh firing rack and insert it into the cool kiln with a firing fork. Follow regular firing instructions until the glass edges appear to be slightly rounded, 1350°–1400°F. Finally, close the vents and let the kiln cool.

To complete the bracelet, drill small holes in the wood links that have been cut and polished; join them alternately to the wire loops of the fused glass rectangles with silver jump rings. Use regular jewelry clasps on the ends of the bracelet or make your own with silver wire or sheet.

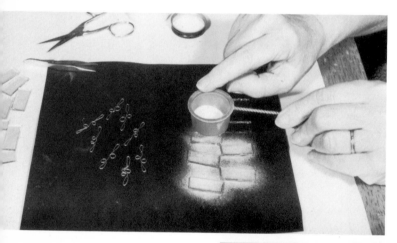

GLASS AND WOOD BRACELET

Glass flux is sifted over half the glass links.

Position small wire hangers on the glass with a pair of tweezers. A dab of Elmer's Glue-all will hold them in place. When each wire is covered with a second glass piece, they are positioned on a slice of insulation brick covered with whiting and kiln wash and placed in a cool kiln.

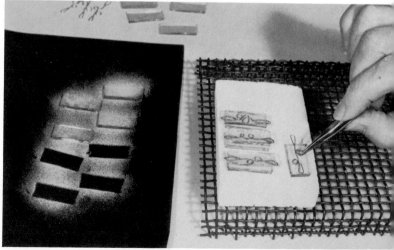

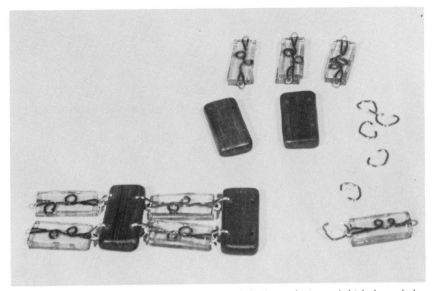

After firing, to complete the bracelet, join polished wood pieces (which have holes drilled in them) to the wire loops of the fused glass units with jump rings.

Units such as these fused links can be combined to make all sorts of jewelry, alone or combined with other materials.

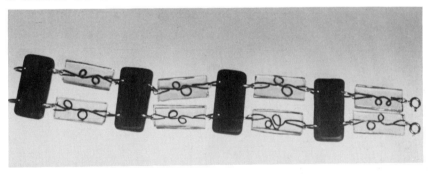

GLASS AND WOOD PENDANT

Three glass units in red and yellow stained glass have single silver loops to combine with wood for a pendant.

They are fired on insulation brick.

Laminated glass and wire "drops" combined with polished walnut and a leather thong.

LAMINATED WIRE DESIGNS

Laminated wire has been discussed chiefly as it is used for wire loop hangers. It can also be effective for larger designs. Fine silver is the best kind of wire for decorative laminations. It almost always retains its clean silver color, although when it is combined with pink glass or pink powdered glass colors, it turns an attractive gold. It may turn a copper color when it is combined with yellow glass. Reds should be tested; they are unpredictable. Sterling silver or nichrome wire turn a dull gray when they are laminated, which does not matter too much when they are used for hangers, but they are disappointing as decorative laminations. Copper wire will turn black before it fuses to the glass because of heavy oxidation in the heat of the kiln. All wire works best if it is lightly tapped and flattened. Avoid flattening it at the point where it passes from between the glass layers. It can become weakened if it is bent frequently and it may break. The bubbles that tend to form around the small wires in a lamination can be most attractive.

Cast silver combined with glass links and silver wire loops in a bracelet. Maurice Rothenberg.

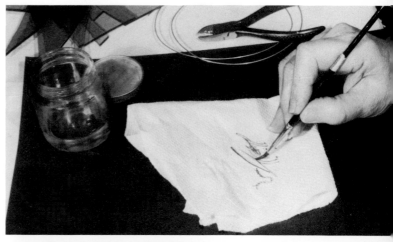

To clean wire for lamination, brush it with alcohol or lighter fluid over paper toweling. 18–20 gauge wire is suitable for decorative lamination, 18-gauge or two twisted strands of thinner wire for loops.

Pick up wires with tweezers, touch them with a bit of glue, and position them on the glass.

Sift glass flux over the wires. It will assist fusing.
Cover it with a second glass.

The pendant was fired to 1425°F to completely
round the glass edges and fuse the wires. Interesting bubbles have formed around angles
in the wires. Blue cathedral glass.

A pendant of laminated wires in window glass
colored with pink glass ice. Fired to 1425°F.

Fused glass and wire units with macramé and woven collars. Bette Warner.

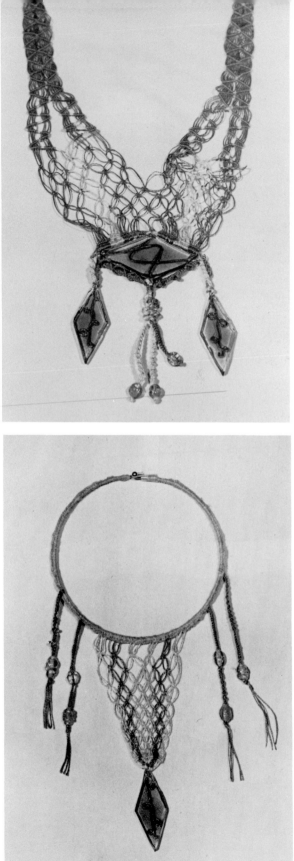

Woven collar and earrings with fused glass and silver wire. By Bette Warner.

CRUSHED GLASS FUSED TO ENAMELED COPPER *

Pieces of stained glass fused to enameled copper must be quite small and of fairly uniform size to fuse successfully. For good results, the glass should fuse at temperatures compatible with the melting temperature of the enamel. Cathedral glass (commercial stained glass) fuses to enamel at about 1400°F. The crushed glass applied to the illustrated pendants is blue and green cathe-

* See *Metal Enameling* by Polly Rothenberg. Crown Publishers Arts and Crafts Series.

dral glass. For the demonstration pendant design, transparent turquoise enamel is wet-packed and fused over silver foil with overglaze accents of fine-line black painted with a very small brush.

A preformed slightly convex round copper shape is selected for the pendant. Convex shapes are not likely to flex and fracture the glass while it is cooling. Cut a hole near the edge for the jump ring to fasten through; then scour the copper and rinse it well. A thick coat of enamel must be fired to the back of the copper disc. This counter-enamel will hold the metal from flexing when crushed glass is fired to the top side. Paint or spray the back of the disc with enameling gum and sift 80-mesh enamel over it. Dry and fire this counter-enamel, then clean the top surface of firescale and apply enamel flux to it. Fire the enamel before crushed glass is applied.

Free-form pieces of silver foil are cut out between leaves of thin tracing paper and are pierced all over with a needle, right through the tracing paper. These holes will let gases escape when the foil is fired and will help keep the foil flat. It may rise up in a few places while it is firing, but if it has been pierced, it will soon flatten again. Brush enameling gum over the enameled surface. Pick up the foil pieces with a damp brush, then press them into position on the pendant surface. Press moisture from the foil with a tissue and let it dry. Fire the piece at 1400°F until the foil is red hot and flat. When it has cooled, wet-pack *transparent* enamel over the foil areas; dry and fire them. After they are cool, it is time to prepare the crushed glass.

Glass must be crushed against a firm surface. A piece of cabinet top with a laminated plastic surface, such as Formica, makes an excellent surface for crushing glass. Formica board remnants are usually obtained at cabinetmaker or woodworking shops. Place some pieces of one color of cathedral glass between folds of heavy canvas and pound them with a hammer to break them up. Protect your eyes and hands from sharp glass segments; never scoop up crushed glass with bare hands! Some of the crushed glass and enameling gum are mixed together in a small container. Pick out the large pieces of glass, leaving only the very small bits for this project. Spoon the glass and gum mixture onto the edge of the pendant surface with a small spatula, patting it down firmly.

The next important step is to sift glass flux enamel or ice over the crushed glass. Flux will bind the glass particles together and assist the fusing process. After a final light spraying with diluted enameling gum, the pendant is dried and fired at 1400°F or until the glass particles are fused together. Do not overfire it. Turn off the kiln and open vents to allow the temperature to drop to 1000°F before you close the door or peepholes and let the kiln cool naturally. If painted black lines are added, they are fired to only 1100°F. When the pendant is completed and has cooled, the edge can be cleaned of firescale by a gentle rubbing with fine steel wool. Care must be taken lest protruding glass is struck and broken off when the copper edge is polished. If all procedures are followed carefully, the glass will not fracture.

Cathedral glass is crushed between layers of heavy canvas, with a ball peen hammer.

A preformed convex round copper shape is enameled on both surfaces with clear metal-enamel or glass flux. Brush the pendant with enameling gum and position the silver foil shapes on the enameled surface. When dry, fire to 1400°F to *fuse* the silver.

Black overglaze lines are applied last and fired to 1000°F.

The pendant's loop is turned back with round-nosed jewelry pliers. Light transparent turquoise and blue.

Wet pack or sift transparent turquoise enamel over the foil. It can be fired separately or with the crushed glass. Very fine pieces of the crushed glass are mixed with gum (agar or any enameling gum) and the mixture is packed around the edge of the pendant. When dry, fire it to 1450°F to fuse and round the glass bits.

When the pendant is completed, metal for a handmade loop (jump ring) is cut from 18- or 20-gauge copper. Cut the small copper segment narrow enough to go through the hole that was drilled through the copper disk near its edge, before it was enameled. When you have cleaned and polished it with fine steel wool to remove rough edges, thread it through the hole and bend it to shape with jewelry pliers.

JEWELRY MADE FROM GLASS SEGMENTS

Flashlight lenses are fused for the demonstrated glass pendant. The smaller lens was fractured between two layers of canvas. The larger lens was brushed with enameling gum, and clear glass flux was sifted in a thin layer. After the pieces of the smaller lens were positioned on it, gum was sprayed and yellow *high-fire* glass ice and yellow transparent enamel were sifted over all. A pinch of opaque black in the center sharpened the design. Because of the hardness of the lens glass, firing was to 1600°F.

Two flashlight lenses were combined for a simple crushed-glass designed pendant. The smaller of the lenses was fractured with blows of the hammer. The pieces of glass are glued to the larger disc; one small piece is laid over a wire loop hanger.

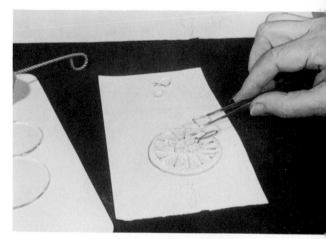

Glass flux and bright yellow transparent enamel are sifted over the entire assemblage. Bits of opaque black enamel are sprinkled in the center. Colors are high-fire.

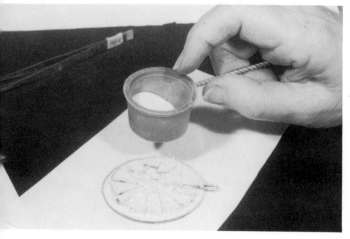

Lucky blows on the smaller glass disc made this interesting fracture. Because of the hardness of flashlight lenses, firing was 1600°F.

Small pieces of colored glass make wonderful "jewels" for pendants and other jewelry. They are fired to 1400°F to just blunt the edges; when fired to 1450°F the glass draws up to round the edges more fully; when fired to 1500°F, the glass becomes cabochon or fully rounded. After they are fired, brush all mica off their base. Residue of mica can prevent fusion or bonding. Shards and other fragments of glass make charming small suspensions and pendants when they are sifted with glass colorants and fused together.

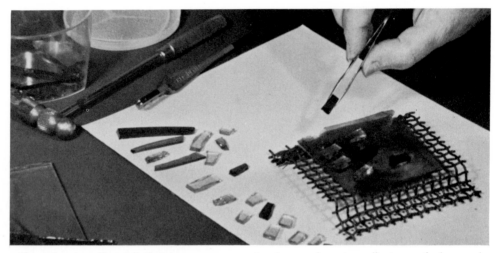

To make glass "jewels" that have many uses in glass work, cut small pieces of glass and spread them on a sheet of mica placed on a mesh trivet for firing.

Test panel for stained glass jewels. *Left to right:* 1. Unfired glass; 2. pieces fired to 1400°F.; 3. pieces fired to 1450°F.; 4. pieces fired to 1500°F.

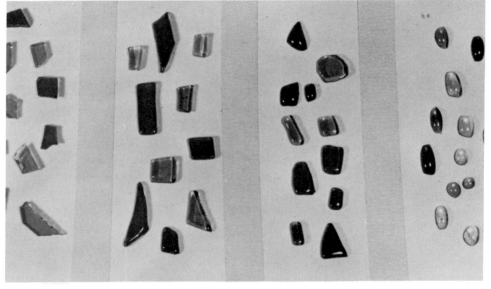

1   2   3   4

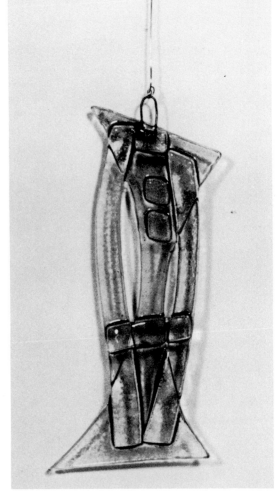

Segments of window glass with siftings of blue transparent enamels and ices fused together in one firing.

Fused pendant. BoBo Zinn. Enamels were fired on a sheet of single-strength window glass. Small rectangles of the colored glass were fused with clear glass. 2″ X 4″. *Photo by Drew Henery.*

JEWELRY FROM TUMBLED GLASS

A most exciting method of preparing small segments of thick antique slab glass for jewelry making is to tumble facet chips or larger chunks in a lapidary tumbler. Pieces as large as walnuts are easily polished in a small "beginner's" tumbler. The glass chunks are tumbled through the regular succession of rock tumbling grits to a final mix of tin oxide, cork, and water for a lovely satiny gloss. The glass is combined with metals or other materials just like any polished stones.

Chips of faceted glass before they were tumbled *(left)*. After tumbling *(right)*.

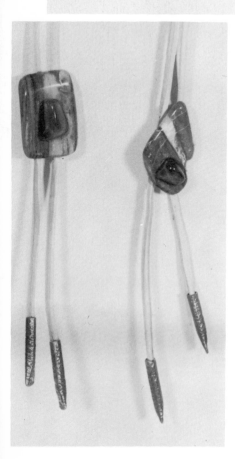

Bolos. Polished stones with tumbled glass lumps epoxied to them. Hand-formed and tooled bolo tips. Maurice Rothenberg.

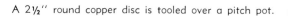

A 2½'' round copper disc is tooled over a pitch pot.

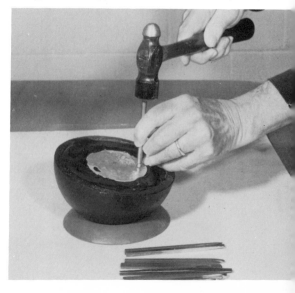

Four wire "posts" are flattened and soldered into four drilled holes. They serve as prongs to hold the glossy tumbled glass nugget. Bright turquoise on copper. Maurice Rothenberg.

Amber tumbled glass with twisted and hammered copper wire. Maurice Rothenberg.

Pendant. Audrea Kreye. Ruby red transparent segment of dalle glass, tumbled and wrapped with electroplated copper wire.

Pendant. Audrea Kreye. Tumbled segment of blue dalle glass with 24-gauge wire macramé and feathers.

Pendant. Audrea Kreye. Blue glass with electroplating directly on the glass.

Silver collar with electroplated emerald green glass nuggets. Audrea Kreye. Audrea is a talented silversmith and enamelist.

7

Blown Glass

THE invention of blown glass, developed at the beginning of the Christian era, was without a doubt one of man's finest achievements. We do not know exactly how nor where it was discovered that molten glass could be blown into a bubble; but it revolutionized glass forming. Every facet of man's life today involves blown glass: science, industry, medicine, construction, containers (seven million tons of them), electronics, and visual art. As a direct aesthetic form created entirely by the individual artist, it is receiving a phenomenal acceptance as a serious sculptural medium. Fluid free blown glass is barely at the threshold of its artistic development. Dozens of colleges and universities are establishing glassworking facilities in their regular art programs.

"Glass blowing," as discussed in this book, means taking a gather of hot glass from a furnace and manipulating it on the end of a metal blowpipe, as distinguished from "lampworking," or starting with a glass tube, one end of which is heated with a torch and becomes the softened and manipulated glass object. A blowpipe (also called a blowing iron or rod) is an iron or steel tube four to six feet long with a tapered end or nose of heatproof alloy. The bore, which is the interior lengthwise cavity of the blowpipe, is about 1/4 inch across. The diameter of the blowing rod's nose is usually selected according to the personal preference of the blower, although too large a nose may gather too much glass, resulting in a thick form and a waste of glass.

◀

#6. David Hopper. Two off-hand blown, hot-tooled white glass figures, each composed of two parts joined with epoxy. From the "American Glass Now" exhibition. *Photo by courtesy of The Toledo Museum of Art.*

Many kinds of glass for offhand blowing are made by mixing and liquefying exactly proportioned materials according to a formula whose basic ingredient is pure silica sand. Silica by itself is difficult to melt and work; it must be modified by other chemicals such as soda (Na_2O) and sometimes potash (K_2O), lime (CaO), and others, along with coloring oxides if colored glass is to be used. These modifications make silica glass more workable and give it a predictable working temperature as well as achieve other desirable qualities. The dry batch mix, compounded according to the purpose for which the glass is to be used, along with some glass cullet of the same kind, is fed into a white-hot melting furnace. When the mass fuses and begins to flow, some impurities rise to the top. Refractory rings may be anchored in a position near the working hole. They float on the molten glass surface, excluding scum from the glass that is being gathered from within the rings.

In a large operation, the impurities that rise to the top of the huge "continuous tank" are held back by a bridge wall that allows the clean glass to flow beneath it through a submerged opening into a clean glass area. From an opening above the clean glass level, glassworkers may gather glass for hand manipulation and blowing, or it may flow into forehearths where it is fed into forming machines. In such a complex operation, glassworkers organized into small groups of six or seven men work together from one reheating furnace or "glory hole." The glassworker who extracts molten glass from the furnace on the end of a blowing iron carefully heats the pipe's nose before inserting it into the molten glass in the furnace. It must be heated to a dull red, just hot enough for the glass to adhere, but not so hot that the glass slides off the iron. The blowpipe is held horizontal in both hands, then tilted downward until its tip just touches the surface of the glass. As it is rotated, it is moved slightly in a horizontal direction away from the direction of rotation, which brings a

Roman Bartkiw gathers glass on his blowing iron. Roman heads the Glass Design Department of Georgian College of Applied Arts and Technology in Barrie, Ontario.

flow of molten glass over the nose of the blowing iron and winds up a gather of glass without collecting unwanted bubbles. After at least one or two full rotations, the pipe is withdrawn from the furnace. The hot glass is a soft viscous mass that must be controlled by continuous rotation of the blowing iron, during and after its removal from the furnace, to prevent the force of gravity from pulling it off the iron. The gatherer must know just how much glass he will need; he must avoid trapping unwanted air bubbles; and he must obtain a symmetrical gather.

When the first gather has been taken from the furnace, it may be rolled on a steel-topped table, to cool it slightly, and "marvered," or rolled, into a cylindrical shape; or the glass-worker may move very quickly to his bench, position the blowing iron across its arms (all the while rotating the iron), pick up a wet scoop-shaped wooden "block" from a tub of water near the bench and shape a sphere from the hot glass while he works it to the end of the rotating blowing iron. While he manipulates the hot material, he sits close against the side of his bench. One hand keeps the iron rotating while the other hand gently cradles the glass with the block. The glass gather rides on a cushion of steam rising from the wet wood block, not on the bare wood.

Marvering, or blocking, the molten glass has cooled it down just enough for a skin of glass to form on the sphere, and it is against this skin that the first bubble of air is blown. Now with just the right amount of molten glass on the blowing iron, with gentle puffs of breath, the blower traps air inside the glass. Because the blowing iron will be returned to the furnace to pick up a second gather, the first bubble must be small, Too large a bubble in the first gather will result in a very thin layer of glass around the bubble. The thin glass may melt off when the second gather is taken from the furnace. It is important to cool the surface of the first gather after the bubble has been blown, so slightly stiffened glass will give stability to the second gather, but not so cool it can break off the iron.

The hot glass is a soft viscous mass that must be controlled by continuous rotation of the blowing iron, during and after its removal from the furnace, to prevent gravity from pulling it off the blowpipe.

A glassworker's bench is simple and functional. The shelf at one side of the bench holds handle-shears, with blades that form opposing right angles that can hold or guide the punty into place or cut off masses of viscous glass; steel-bladed jacks and other forming tools are arranged in convenient order to be readily accessible. Wooden blocks in a tub or bucket of water are at hand when needed.

Blocking the molten glass has cooled it down just enough for a "skin" of glass to form on the gather. With gentle puffs of breath, Roman traps air inside the glass in a small bubble.

As soon as the second gather is taken from the furnace, it is blocked again and inflated further. With a doubled tong called a jack, or pucella, the glassworker may grove or neck his glass by circling it just beyond the blowpipe's nose. Periodically, the glass is returned to the reheating furnace so it is kept hot enough to be necked, worked, shaped, or trimmed with glass shears while it is pliable. A great part of a glassworker's time is spent in warming up his material and cooling down his work. To achieve a form of larger size, additional gathers and blockings must be made, one over the other. Subsequent manipulation depends upon the kind of glass article to be made. Gravity exerting its pull stretches the glass. Sometimes it is swung back and forth while it is still hot and flexible to bring the glass lower on the blowing iron or to elongate it. At this point it may be lowered into a waiting mold. It may be flattened by spinning or shaped with moist wooden paddles. The wood blocks and tools are made from apple, cherry, or other wood that does not cause sap problems.

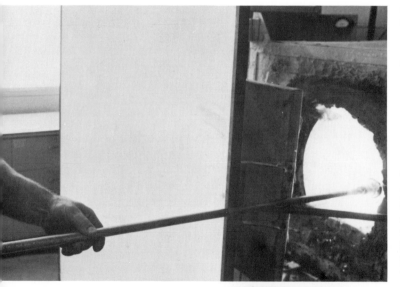

Periodically the glass is returned either to the furnace to gather more glass or to the reheating furnace (glory hole) to keep it hot and pliant enough to be worked, necked, shaped, or trimmed.

The base of a form may be flattened in one of several ways. Roman taps the hot glass with the end of a jack. He sits close against the side of his bench; his left hand continues rotating the blowpipe to prevent the hot soft glass from sagging.

Artist David Lucas holds a punty with a hot glass trailing for Roman to manipulate onto the form.

When the blowing and preliminary shaping are achieved, the glass is cooled slightly so the partly formed piece can be transferred to a four-foot solid pontil rod (punty) tipped with a small bit of hot glass. The tip of the punty is heated a dull red before the bit of glass is gathered, but it must not get so hot that the glass form will melt off it. The hot bit of molten glass is marvered or pulled into a point that is pressed against the center of the bottom on the blown glass bubble. Once the punty is attached to the blown glass piece opposite the blowing iron juncture, the glass is chilled with water at the point where it was grooved (necked) after the second gather. The point of intended severance is scratched with a large file or small handsaw; the glassworker raps the blowing rod, *not the glass object,* and the glass is cracked off the iron's tip. Now that the glass is free of the blowing iron and attached at its opposite end to the punty, it is again inserted into the reheating furnace just far enough to heat it without overheating the punty. After each manipulation of the glass, the form must be returned to the furnace for reheating.

All the separate portions of the glass form are joined and shaped with shears and simple tools. For decorative work, extra small gathers of hot glass from the furnace are applied with another punty. The ragged edge of the glass form where it was separated from the blowing iron is reheated by being inserted into the furnace just far enough to heat the glass edge red-hot. When it is returned to the bench, it may be opened with a wet tool, trimmed with glass shears, stretched into a necked form or spread into a more open form while the glass is still pliable. The skillful finisher knows just how to utilize the pull of gravity to maintain clean flowing lines on the glass form. The completed hot glass object is removed from the punty with a gentle blow to the rod; it falls on an asbestos bed or asbestos-covered pronged fork and is quickly inserted into the annealing lehr where it remains until all strain is removed from the glass as described under "Annealing Glass."

David scores the glass with a saw preparatory to severing it from the iron.

Under Roman's watchful eyes, David cracks off the glass form with a sharp blow to the rod. With asbestos gloves, he will transfer it immediately to an annealing oven.

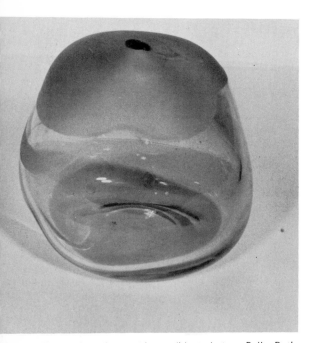

Blown glass open form with palladium luster fired later to 1000°F. Polly Rothenberg.

Blown glass form with sandblast design. Polly Rothenberg.

SMALL MARMOT. Blown bubble with bottom plane ground and polished. Green jeweled eyes epoxied. Polly Rothenberg.

Although the methods described concern glassworking in a large operation, the series of processes in a small one- or two-man situation are similar but adapted to a greatly modified scale. The independent craftsman dedicated to working creatively today must plan a strict disciplinary routine for himself because of the very high temperatures involved. Once a familiarity with proved and safe glassblowing procedures is acquired, the artist is free to explore the tantalizing world of molten glass. The art of glassworking is evolving at an exciting pace today. A phenomenon of the current resurgent interest in blown glass is the burgeoning number of individual glassworkers who either maintain their own studios and equipment or who work independently in a college workshop after class hours. On these pages are illustrations of some of these talented professional artists at work along with the astonishing variety of their glass forms. Because off-hand blown glass sculpture is an important development of our time, examples of these sculptural works are shown in this special blown glass section rather than with the glass sculpture and architectural glass group.

ROMAN BARTKIW HAND-BLOCKS
A BLOWN GLASS BUBBLE

The glass craftsman who is experienced in glassblowing can achieve subtle variations in a blown form by "hand-blocking" it with a soaked folded wet newspaper. The conventional wood blocks are used in conjunction with this interesting process, before or during the wet paper blocking process. The folded paper is fully soaked before the blocking begins. Because the hot glass bubble is cradled on a layer of rising steam, the paper (12 to 16 layers) does not catch fire. This method is recommended only for the experienced glassblower.

Roman Bartkiw demonstrates daily in his glass workshop. He blocks the glass with wet newspaper. Heat does not penetrate to his hand; the glass form rides on a layer of steam. The paper is quite wet.

The glass is reheated and blocked gently from the end. The shape of the form can be felt through the wet paper, which does not burn.

Roman may alternate blocking with a wood block if he feels the form may require it. He continually reheats the glass.

Back to the newspaper and more manipulation of the glass form.

With the wet folded newspaper, subtle contours are defined that are not possible with a wooden block. The paper is somewhat tattered at this point. Additional refinements may be made with tools, but the form subtleties are retained. All photographs of Georgian College activities in the Glass Design Department were taken by Marc Robillard.

Artist Robin Clarke grinds the base of her blown glass form. Water drips on the rotating grinder stone from a long tapered trough. Georgian College.

The glass is held firmly. Eyes must be kept on the form as the wheel rotates, for the slightest movement of the hand can change the glass position and scar the smooth glass surface.

The ground surface is refined with sand belts from coarse to fine. Final polishing is achieved with a cork belt. The belts are kept on numbered pegs.

MODERN GLASS OVENS AND SOME WOOD BLOCKS

Although glass is blown today in much the same way it was formed centuries ago, there are some modern gas and oil furnaces and ovens for the glassworker who is not interested in constructing them. The wooden blocks, mostly hand formed, are still like those primitive ones. Other forming tools are shown in use in accompanying illustrations.

Reheating furnace, or "glory hole." Courtesy A. D. Alpine, Inc.

Although many glassworkers build their own furnaces, glassblowing equipment is available on the market now. A gas-fired glass tank melting furnace, constructed of pure zircon firebrick. Movable stand for blowpipe and punties. Designed for studio artists and schools. *Photo courtesy of A. D. Alpine, Inc., California.*

Annealing oven, or lehr (lare), of welded sheet steel, lined with 4½'' firebrick insulation. Courtesy A. D. Alpine, Inc.

Wooden block of cherrywood for shaping blown glass.

Cherrywood shaping paddle.

Wood mold for pressing blown glass forms.

A.

C.

B.

D.

A. Three-dimensional layered stained glass. Fredrica Fields.

B. Blown glass vase. John Nickerson. Artist in residence, Blenko Glass Company.

C. **RED JEWEL.** Edris Eckhardt. Bronze cast over glass relief sculpture.

D. Hand-formed silver collar with electroplated stained glass nuggets. Audrea Kreye.

A.

A. Section of 65-foot faceted glass skylight in California mart of Los Angeles. By the Glassart Studio.
B. Stained glass mosaic table top. Polly Rothenberg.
C. Fused stained-glass wind chimes with weathered walnut. Polly Rothenberg.

B.

C.

A.

B.

A. Lighted Farbigem bonded glass sculptures. Van Tetterode Studio, Amsterdam, Holland. *Courtesy of Willet Studio.*

B. Bent glass sculpture. Louis La Rooy, for Willet Stained Glass Studios.

A.

A. **STONEY PATH.** Edward J. Byrne. Leaded and painted stained glass powder-room window. Carnwath residence.
B. One panel of Farbigem bonded mural wall, *World History of Medicine*. Willet Studio. Installed in the Ohio State University Medical Center.

B.

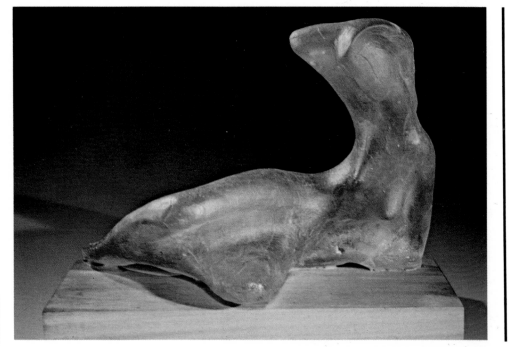

A.

B.

A. **PINK NUDE.** Edris Eckhardt. Cast glass.
B. **HOLY FAMILY.** Don Shepherd. Cast glass relief sculpture.

A. **FLOWERS.** Old Dominion Stained Glass Studio. Leaded antique glass. *Courtesy, Blenko Glass Company.*
B. Suspended panel. Edward J. Byrne. Leaded stained glass.

A.

B.

A.

A. **CREATION.** Laws Stained
   Glass Studio. Faceted glass
   in epoxy resin matrix. *Cour-
   tesy, Blenko Glass Company.*
B. Three-dimensional layered
   stained glass. Fredrica
   Fields. *Photo by Kenneth
   Fields.*

B.

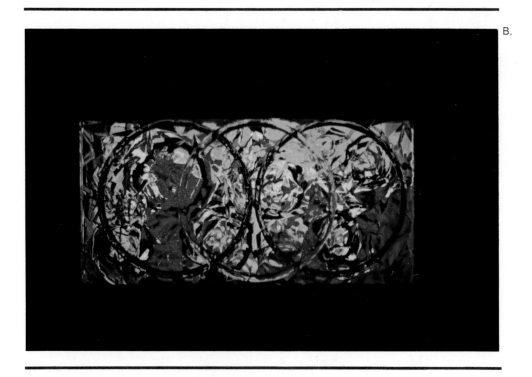

A.

B.

A. Leaded antique glass butter-
   fly. Polly Rothenberg.
B. Blown glass bottle with tooled
   design. Steven Zachofsky.
C. Antique glass lantern. Bette
   Warner.

C.

VERNON BREJCHA'S WORK AND PHILOSOPHY

"Annually, as the hot south wind is forming waves over the golden high plains, I return to the flat lands for the wheat harvest. Atop the grain combine, one's hands have to become a part of the machine. The Kansas sun shows no mercy as the grain flows into the bin as if it were a yellow liquid. Over the constant roar of the engine, chains, belts and gears, the ear tries to detect how the grain and straw are separating.

"The roar is not too different from the burners on a glass tank as the melt gives off an intense heat like the prairie sun. Here the hands tune themselves to primitive tools to master another golden flowing liquid—molten glass giving off light only for the artist to enjoy before it stiffens into a statement that had to be made."—Vernon Brejcha

Vase and bowl. Vernon Brejcha. Clear glass with copper blue applied designs. Vase 8½" tall. Bowl 6" diameter.

TORNADO CLOUD. Vernon Brejcha. Blown glass wall sculpture. 11" X 19".

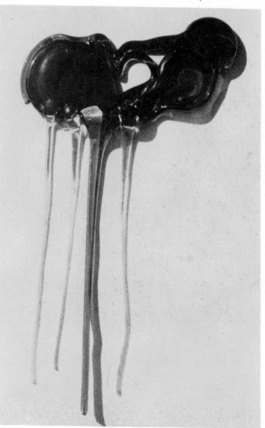

PRAIRIE STORM. Vernon Brejcha. Blown glass with gray plate glass. 13" X 17".

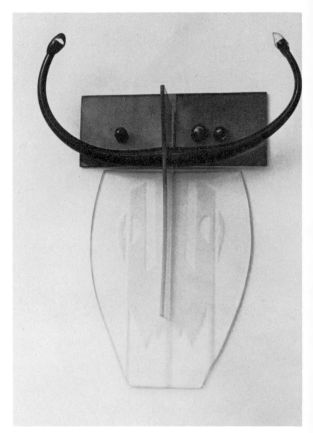

WHY THE BUFFALO! Vernon Brejcha. Wall sculpture of blown and plate glass with sandblasting. 16" X 17" X 5".

ONE LAST TROPHY FOR JACKSON SUNDOWN. Vernon Brejcha. Glass wall sculpture of mirror, blown glass, gray plate glass with sandblasting. 20" X 24".

VERNON BREJCHA
GLASS BLOWING

The first gather of glass is marvered (blocked).

The gather is inflated with gentle
puffs of breath.

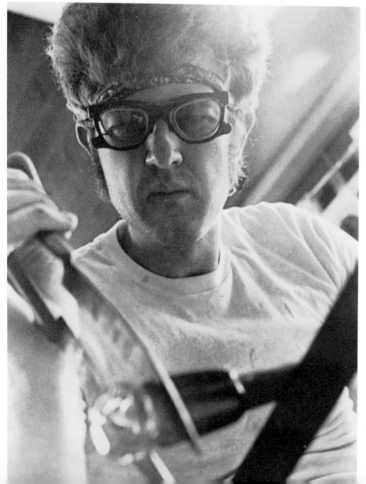

Vernon Brejcha necks the first
gather of clear glass. The clear
glass will stay warmer on the pipe
than the black glass that will case
the bubble.

A second gather is cradled in a wet wood block. Blocking is very important. The glass is red hot.

The bubble grows in size from repeated gathers and blowings. The third gather is blocked. It is a very gentle process, with little if any pressure being applied. The dark area on the bubble indicates that it is cooling toward the pipe end first.

With extra glass on the punty, a design is threaded on the bubble.

Vernon can work alone when necessary. He gathers a bit of glass on the end of a punty.

The punty is attached to the base of the glass form.

With a blow to the pipe, he breaks off the bubble.

He returns the glass to the fire and inserts it into the furnace just far enough to heat the open end until it is red, but not so far as to collapse the bubble.

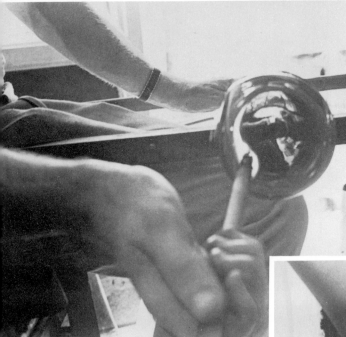

Pressing with a wet wood stick in his right hand, he opens the glass into a bowl form as his left hand rotates the iron.

While the glass is still very hot, it is broken off the punty into the annealing oven.

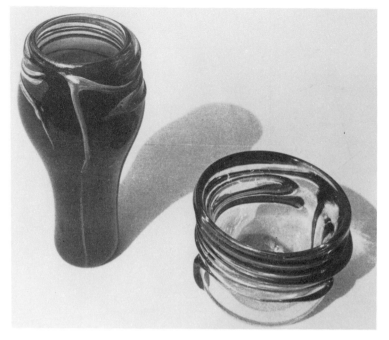

Blown vase and bowl with applied glass designs. Vernon Brejcha.

WALL FLOWER. Vernon Brejcha. Blown and plate glass wall sculpture. 10½" X 15".

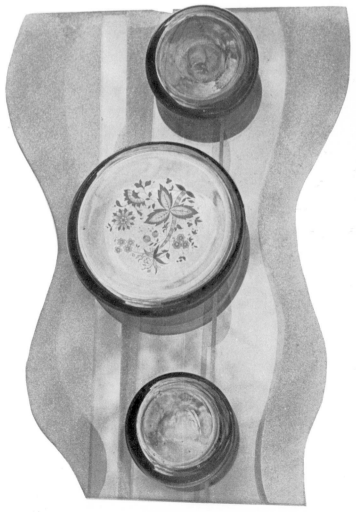

VERNON BREJCHA DEMONSTRATES
BLOWING A GLASS GOBLET

Gathers are taken for Vernon's demonstration of blowing a glass goblet. All
photos of Vernon Brejcha's work are by
Sherry Brejcha.

Blocking the second gather.

Vernon makes decorative cuts at the
base of a hot bubble.

He adds a small bit of color between two of the decorative cuts.

Glass is added, pulled out to the desired length and cut off to make a stem.

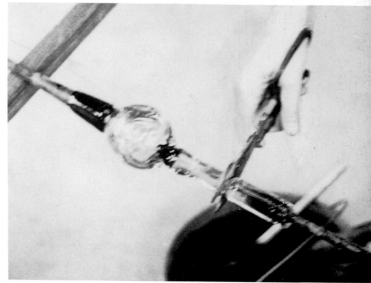

The stem is added to a hot paddy of glass to make a foot.

Glass is added to attach the punty to the foot of the goblet.

After the punty is attached, the neck is broken from the blowpipe with a light tap to the pipe. Where the glass was separated from the pipe, it is reheated in the furnace and it is opened with a wet stick.

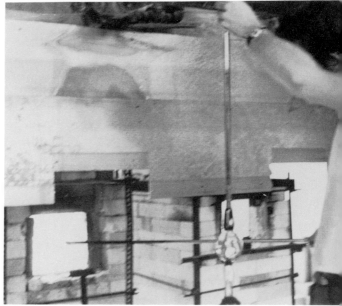

The completed goblet. Dark areas are green. The cup of the goblet is amber with trailings of color. Stem is clear glass. 7½'' tall. In the author's collection. Vernon Brejcha is Assistant Professor of Art at Tusculum College, Greeneville, Tennessee. *Photos by Sherry Brejcha.*

SOME OF TODAY'S GLASS ARTISTS AND BLOWN GLASS WORKS THAT APPEARED IN THE "AMERICAN GLASS NOW" EXHIBITION

Off-hand blown forms. Kim Newcomb. Bottle with applied decoration and fumed surface, 11" X 3⅝" X 3⅝". Vase with applied decoration and fumed surface, 6½" X 4⅛" X 4⅛". Bowl with applied foot and fumed surface, 7½" X 5⅛" X 5⅛". From the "American Glass Now" exhibition. *Photo by courtesy of The Toledo Museum of Art.*

JUMPING TROUT. Kim Newcomb. Off-hand blown glass with applied glass parts.

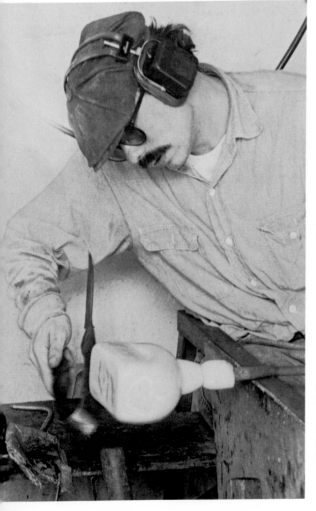

Kim Newcomb works on one of his blown glass Bread Bottle forms while listening to FM radio. He feels the rhythm of the music inspires a rhythm in his work. Mr. Newcomb is Assistant Professor of Fine and Applied Arts at the University of Illinois, Urbana-Champaign. *Photo by Jennifer Manning.*

CLUSTERFORM II. Eriks Rudans. Cluster of off-hand blown forms on a base of epoxy-painted fiber glass reinforced polyester. 11½'' X 31'' X 24''. From the "American Glass Now" exhibition. Mr. Rudans teaches at Saint Cloud State College, Saint Cloud, Minnesota. *Photo by courtesy of The Toledo Museum of Art.*

Eriks's workbench and tools after a busy workshop demonstration.

Eriks Rudans during a workshop demonstration.

TRANSFUSION. Curtis C. Hoard. Off-hand blown form
with flocked metal, rubber, Plexiglas, and flocked parts.
12″ X 16½″ X 24¼″. From the "American Glass
Now" exhibition. Mr. Hoard is Associate Professor of
Art, University of Minnesota, Minneapolis. *Photo by
courtesy of The Toledo Museum of Art.*

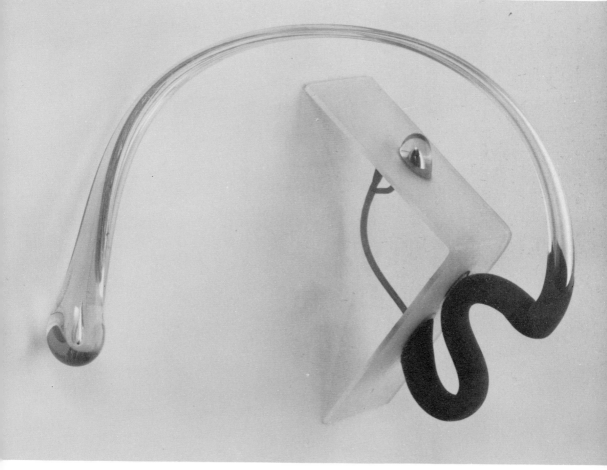

SPACE CUP #4. Michael Cohn. One of a series of nonfunctional cups. Blown, cut, and fabricated glass with sand-blasted contrasting areas. From the collection of Mark Graham, Baltimore.

Blown glass cups. Paula Bartron. Part of a series. *Left to right:* Untitled #13, blown cup with applied foot and handle and fumed surface; Untitled #3, blown cup with trailed decoration and applied handles; Untitled #8, blown cup with applied foot and handle. From the "American Glass Now" exhibition. Courtesy of The Toledo Museum of Art.

VENINI SERIES #1. Marvin B. Lipofsky, assisted by Gianni Toso, Murano, Italy. Off-hand blown, hot-tooled form. 11½'' X 15'' X 17''. From the "American Glass Now" exhibition. *Photo by courtesy of The Toledo Museum of Art.*

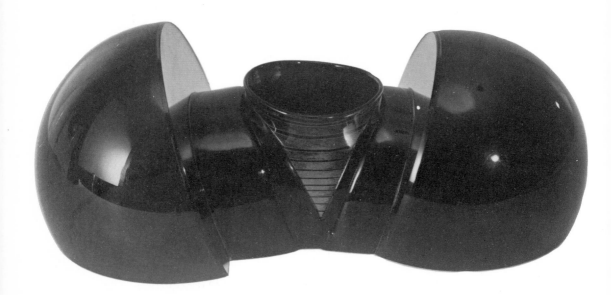

Untitled. Michael Edward Cohn. Blown, cut, and polished glass form with mirrors. 3⅞'' X 10⅞'' X 5½''. From the ''American Glass Now'' exhibition. *Photo by courtesy of The Toledo Museum of Art.*

Glass jar. Kent Ipsen. Off-hand blown jar with trailed surface design. 14'' X 10''. From the ''American Glass Now'' Exhibition. *Photo by courtesy of The Toledo Museum of Art.*

Kent Ipsen constricts a large blown form with a wet wooden jack. Mr. Ipsen is Chairman of the Crafts Department at Virginia Commonwealth University, Richmond.

8
Glass Sculpture and Architectural Art

HISTORY abounds with examples of glass art, but today glass is climbing to notable levels of aesthetic approval as a serious sculptural and architectural art medium. New uses of old methods, such as sandblasting, mirroring, bonding, bending, glassblowing and more, are encouraging further extensive experimentation to discover what else can be done with, to, and on glass. This glamorous material depends for its beauty on the light rays that journey through it and illuminate it with ever-changing effects from moment to moment. Glassworkers, investigating their material in its relation to light, are evolving new and unusual processes to exploit this property. Not only does the sculptor and architectural artist work with light as it directly affects the glass, but also with whatever is seen through the glass, around it and reflected in it, and with the light that illuminates these elements. Although individual artists are finding new ways with glass, the professional glass studios, large and small, with their extensive resources and contacts, actively advance and improve appreciation and understanding of glass art among art lovers, collectors, and the public in general. They enrich the lives of all of us with their devotion to the creation of lasting beauty.

◀

Mosaic Cross. Glassart Studio. Architectural sculpture of antique sheet stained glass and dalle glass with gold lamination. In the United Church of Christ, Scottsdale, Arizona. *Photo by Glassart Studio, Phoenix, Arizona.*

Three-dimensional stained glass. Fredrica Fields. In the main lounge of the YWCA, Greenwich, Connecticut. *Photo by Kenneth Fields.*

◀

MADONNA AND CHILD. Edris Eckhardt. Cast glass in turquoise, aqua, and blue with transparent gold surface touched with rose tones from the copper reduction during fusion. Collection of Gates Mills. *Photo by The Cleveland Museum of Art.*

Three-dimensional stained glass panel. Fredrica Fields. Main lounge of the YWCA, Greenwich, Connecticut. *Photo by Kenneth Fields.*

Three-dimensional stained glass panel. Fredrica Fields. Main lounge of the YWCA, Greenwich, Connecticut. *Photo by Kenneth Fields.*

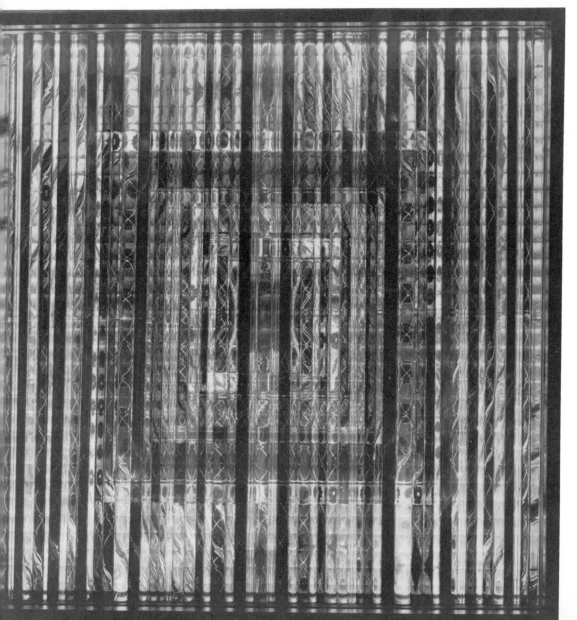

The boxlike frame that holds one of Fredrica's panels is built with reinforced corners. The frame's back edge has strong molding to support the glass. Fitted wood strips along the interior of the frame sides hold the composition secure.

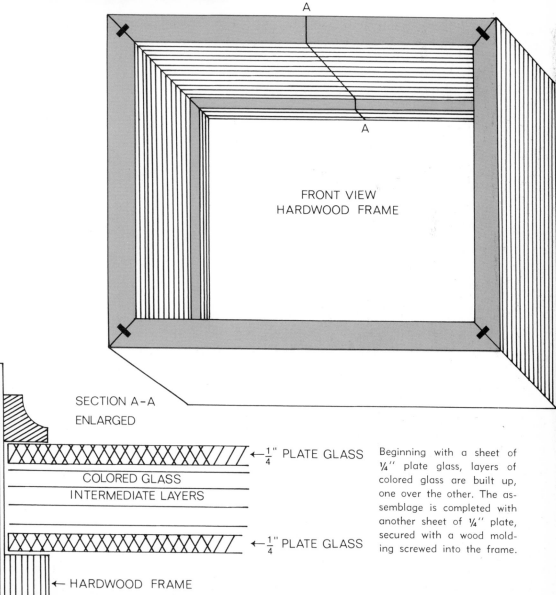

A

A

FRONT VIEW
HARDWOOD FRAME

SECTION A-A
ENLARGED

←$\frac{1}{4}$" PLATE GLASS

COLORED GLASS
INTERMEDIATE LAYERS

←$\frac{1}{4}$" PLATE GLASS

← HARDWOOD FRAME

Beginning with a sheet of $\frac{1}{4}$" plate glass, layers of colored glass are built up, one over the other. The assemblage is completed with another sheet of $\frac{1}{4}$" plate, secured with a wood molding screwed into the frame.

FREDRICA FIELDS'S WORK

The glass of Fredrica Fields is three-dimensional construction in pure glass. She does not in any way change the character or brilliance of the original glass by fusing, bending, or laminating it.

The boxlike frame that holds one of her panels is built with reinforced corners. The frame's back edge has a strong molding to support the glass. Fitted wood strips along the interior of the frame sides hold the composition secure. She lays the hardwood frame with its back edge flat against the top of a strong iron light-table so she may see the composition while she builds up the colorful layers.

Beginning with a sheet of ¼-inch plate glass, layers of colored glass are built up, one over the other. When light is transmitted through these layers it is diffused and refracted into a mélange of color. Fredrica works with an endless variety of glass materials: antique sheet, rods, tubes, marbles, glass rings, jewels, beads, rondels, and faceted glass chips. She designs as she builds, taking apart and putting together each layer many times before she completes the assemblage with another sheet of ¼-inch plate, secured with a wood molding screwed into the frame.

This talented artist comments: "My work is entirely a construction of glass fitted together bit by bit, sometimes solid, sometimes with air spaces, sometimes in layers, but never the same in any two panels. Occasionally, I use commercial epoxy to hold a piece in a certain position, as I do not use leads internally for this purpose. I do use "drop-in" holding frames in the layered work, but they are not visible as they fit the inner contour of the frame that is holding the work. It is a long demanding process—truly a work of love.

"As to colors, I use all colors. They are spattered about; no one color predominates. There is not a green panel, a blue panel, and so on. They are multicolor. Sometimes I use black and white opaque glass in combination; sometimes I make use of engraved flashed glasses. This allows wonderful glints of light and color to come through."—Fredrica Fields

Three-dimensional stained glass interior wall panels in the lobby of the Marie Cole Auditorium, Greenwich Library, Connecticut. Fredrica Fields. *Photos by Kenneth Fields.*

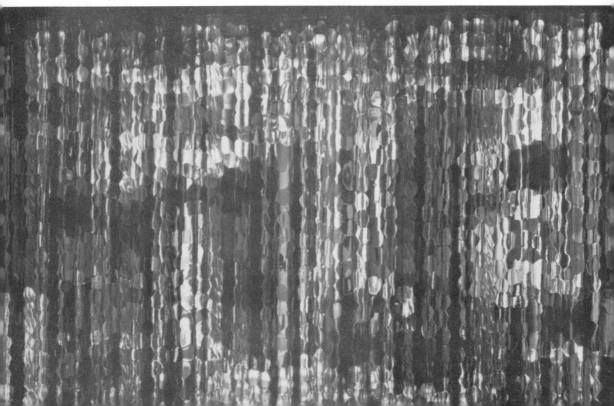

e-dimensional stained glass interior wall panels in the lobby of the Marie Cole Auditorium, Green-
Library, Connecticut. Fredrica Fields. *Photos by Kenneth Fields.*

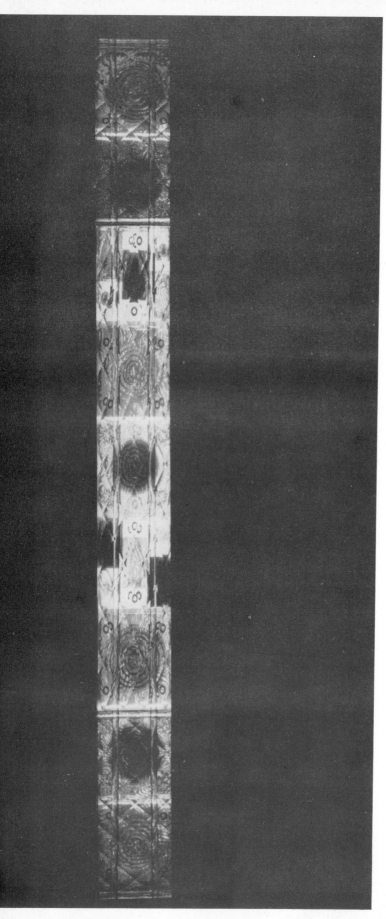

Exhibition Panel. 5″ tall X 5½″ wide.
Fredrica Fields.

Exhibition panel. 20½'' tall X 5'' wide. Fredrica Fields.

WINTER'S NIGHT. Fredrica Fields. Exhibition panel.
17'' tall X 14'' wide. *Photo by Kenneth Fields.*

Exhibition panel. 5½'' tall X 5'' wide. Fredrica Fields.

THE WORK OF LUCIEN DEN AREND

Lucien den Arend of Zwijndrecht, Holland, is an eminent architectural sculptor. The sophisticated appearance of his bent glass work is deceptively simple. With rectangles of glass supported on steel molds that he shapes on a hand roller, he bends the forms in a large kiln.

Lucien says modestly: "I have only to bend the steel; the furnace shapes the glass. I rolled the molds out of 4mm steel and bent the glass on these in the large kiln of Bruining Glass Company in Dordrecht, Holland. For the line, I covered the glass with adhesive vinyl, cut out the space for the line and sandblasted it. The line is rubbed with oil paint."

Lucien den Arend's sculptural work is usually quite large. He is well known in Europe for his environmental sculptures. The glass sculptures shown here will be models for future commissioned work of six to eight feet.

Lucien den Arend inserts the steel sheet into a hand-worked roller. He shapes the first large curve, then reverses the sheet in the roller to form the smaller curves.

Turning the roller to bend the sheet.

The steel sheet must be controlled.

The curves are subtle. Lucien sights the arch of the form.

Applying oil color to the etched line.

Rubbing in the paint.

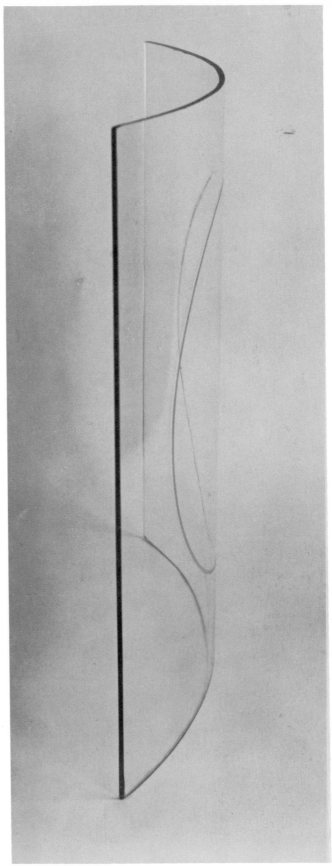

MONOLINEAR I. Lucien den Arend.
¼" bent plate glass. Size before
bending 27" X 26".

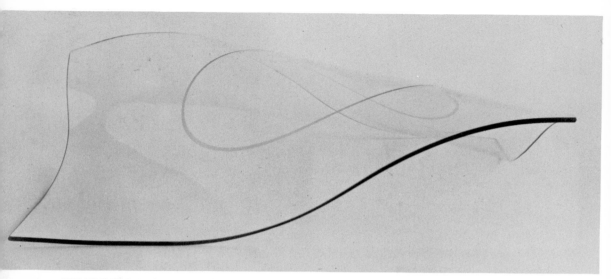

MONOLINEAR II. Lucien den Arend. ¼" bent plate glass. Size before bending 20" X 28".

MONOLINEAR II. Alternate view, with reflection.

CONTOURING GLASS OVER NICHROME WIRE

A new and exciting technique in glass-bending requires 16-gauge or heavier nichrome wire. The demonstration sculpture project "White Peaks" also calls for insulation board such as Ceramiguard, Marinite, or other porous fireproof acoustical board that has been prefired as described under "Molds for Glass Fusing and Bending." Dry kiln wash is sifted over the board, then wires are inserted. Do not push them so far through the board that points of the wire project out the underneath side of the board and cause problems. The nichrome wire lengths are stuck into the board and bent in projecting patterns over which double-strength window glass will be positioned and sagged in the kiln. No pointed ends of the wires should project upward; they should be bent so the glass rests only on curved or horizontal wires. At least three of the tallest bent wire projections should be of nearly equal height to hold the glass sheet horizontal so it does not slide off the wires in the kiln before it can bend.

The next step is very important. Make a thin creamy solution of kiln wash and water, and paint all the nichrome wires wherever the glass can possibly touch them as it slumps in the heat of the kiln. The kiln wash protects the wires from adhering to the glass. Dry the wires before you position glass over them.

The glass should be cut wide enough that it extends beyond the outermost wires farther than the distance between the tops of the wires and the board, if you want some of the glass to flatten out around the perimeter of the composition. When the glass begins to bend in the hot kiln, first the entire sheet bends in a broad shallow arc before it sags between the individual wire projections. The edges of the glass touch the fireproof board and then slump flat, making a base for the sculpture. Glass ices and enamels can be sifted over the flat glass before it is positioned on the wires. (Always clean any glass that will be kiln-fired.)

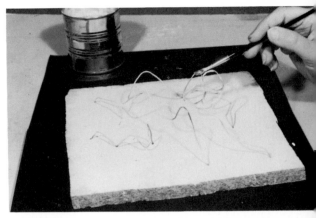

Nichrome wires are given a coating of kiln wash.

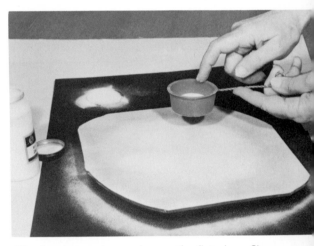

Sift glass ices and enamels over the flat glass. Clear colorless sheet glass can be very attractive when bent like this.

The glass is positioned over the shaped wires.

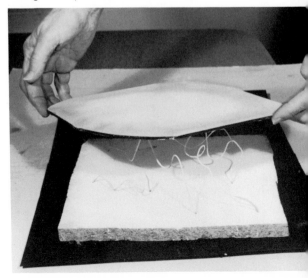

When the glass has been positioned carefully over the assemblage, it is time to insert it into a cool kiln well away from the door if it is a front-loading kiln. Switches are turned to *low* position. *Leave the door vented* one-half inch for an hour, then turn the switches to *high* position until the temperature climbs to 950°F. At that temperature the kiln door is closed. The final firing temperatures are all-important in contouring glass over nichrome wire. The illustrated project, "White Peaks," made of PPG Pennvernon double-strength window glass showed a definite contour at 1250°F. By 1400°F, it had arced and had begun to flatten out around the edges of the glass. It had slumped between the wires as far as desired at 1450°F, and the glass ices and enamels had melted and matured. The kiln was shut off and the door was vented for 2 to 3 minutes to completely halt further softening of the glass; otherwise the softened glass would have continued to stretch over the wires, which could allow them to protrude through the soft glass. Although this could be an interesting development, it would not be the effect that was planned. After brief venting, the kiln door was closed while the glass cooled slowly through the annealing cycle. (See the section "Annealing Glass.")

For a very different nichrome wire proj-

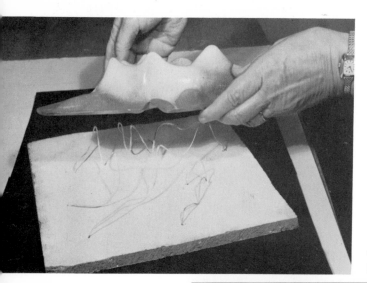

When firing is completed, the glass is lifted off the wires.

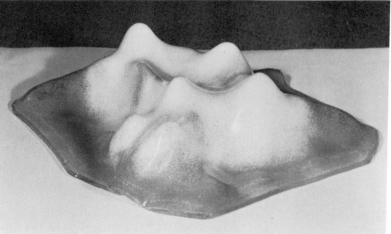

WHITE PEAKS. Polly Rothenberg. Enameled bent glass sculpture.

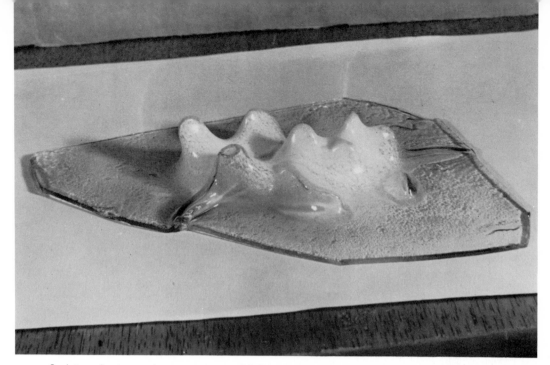

Sculpture fired over the same wires at 25°F higher temperature. The glass has sagged deeper between the wires. One of the wires pushed through the glass. The ragged edge was ground off in an interesting variation.

ect, a three-inch square piece of nichrome mesh, the kind used as a firing rack for copper enameling, is the base for drape-bending glass to form a square tray. Although this is a fascinatingly simple method, it must nonetheless be done precisely to achieve the desired result. Brush a thin creamy solution of kiln wash and water over the mesh and dry it. The square of wire mesh is positioned flat and centered on a thick ceramic kiln-post or a slim section of insulation brick. A five-inch square of clean double-strength window glass, placed on the mesh and extending evenly beyond the edges all around it, must clear the kiln-floor when it sags around the perimeter of the nichrome mesh. The assemblage is positioned on a prefired insulation board and inserted into a cool kiln well away from the kiln door. The switches are turned to *low* position. Follow firing instructions for nichrome wire project "White Peaks" until the temperature reaches 1300°F. Then take a quick look inside the barely opened door (if the kiln is front loading) to check the progress of the bending glass. The glass that extends beyond the edge of the wire mesh will slowly begin

to bend down around the edges in a subtle ripple effect. Just how far you want it to bend is a personal decision. Avoid opening the door very far or too often; the glass nearest the door will not sag as much as the glass around the other three sides of the piece if the door was shut off at 1350°F and the door vented about two minutes for this project. The glass was cooled and annealed.

If your kiln is a top loader, the bending glass is observed through a peephole. There is too great a surge of intense heat into your face when an attempt is made to lift up the lid of a top-loading kiln while it is firing. A first experimental firing could be made by shutting off the switches at 1350°F and removing peephole plugs to halt the rise in temperature, if you have difficulty seeing the glass through a peephole in a top loader. After the fired glass has become cool, it can be refired to a slightly higher temperature for further bending. If you are using nichrome mesh, it is well to halt the bending process before the glass sags to the point that the mesh becomes entrapped and cannot be removed from the glass after it has cooled.

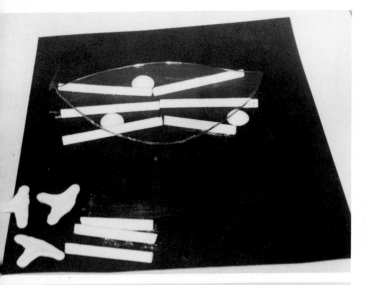

Clay-firing accessories make interesting glass bending designs. They are painted with kiln wash and dried before the glass is positioned over them.

The glass was sifted with yellow glass coloring powder, with brown, orange, and light green spots.

A three-inch square piece of nichrome wire mesh is painted with kiln wash solution for a separator.

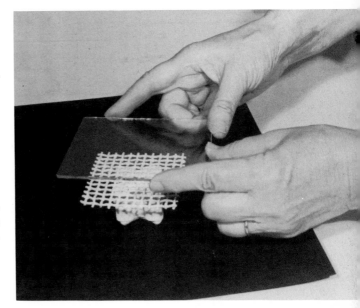

A five-inch square of clean double-strength window glass will clear the kiln floor when it sags around the perimeter of the mesh. It has been raised on small clay stilts.

Units like this can be epoxied to plate glass backgrounds repetitively for dividers.

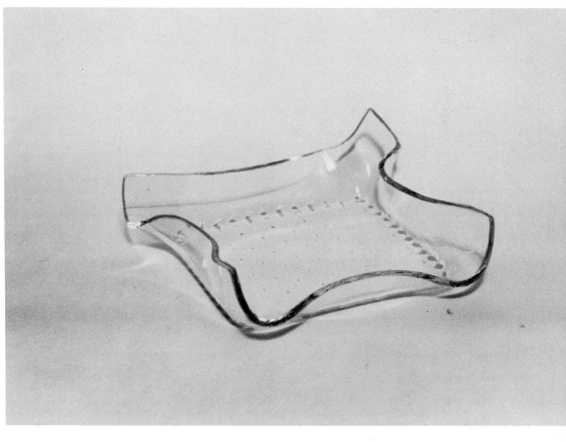

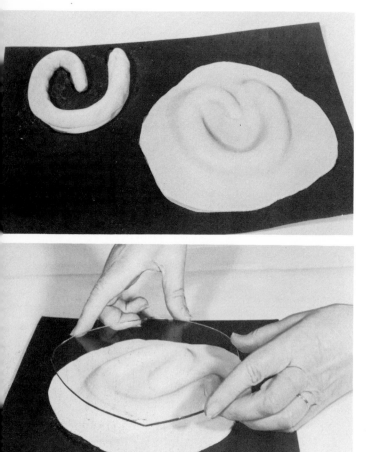

Moist white sculpture clay was rolled out and pressed over a curled clay coil that was leather-hard. The clay form is used for a mold.

Double-strength window glass is cut to a size that will not extend beyond the mold perimeter when it is fired.

The completed sculptural unit.

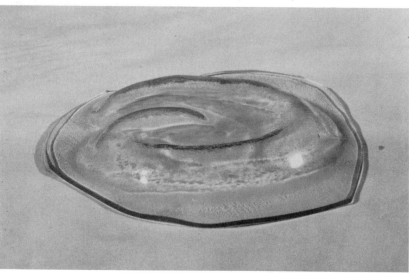

BETH BEEDE'S WORK

Beth Beede's craft designs reflect her years of study and teaching in the far Northwest and in Alaska. Although her work appears in many materials, the best known are her fine designs in fibers and in combinations of glass with other materials. Inspiration for some of her compositions comes from ancient Northwest Indian designs and their historical masks made from carved wood with grasses, walrus whiskers, eagle down, and fibers.

Beth comments on her work in glass: "I feel the possibilities of combining glass and fibers have to do with the contrasts and likenesses between them, for instance, the smooth solid and yet fluid forms of the glass as opposed to the textured, soft suppleness of fibers. The varying degree of permanency between materials has its roots in some of our earliest traditions in Europe, Africa, and the Americas; the use of clay, stone, metal, or glass contrasts with the more perishable materials like dry grasses, hair, fur, feathers, leather, fibers, and wood.

"The reflective qualities of glass and its transparency possibilities, with or without the formation of new colors in transitional areas are really exciting. Even though I feel pulled to natural materials as a satisfying complement of glass, I would be missing a lot if I ignored the possibilities in exploring manmade materials."—Beth Beede.

In her exotic hanging panel, MORNING SUN, Beth combined fused glass with wire, dyed wool, and beads. Two 8-inch single-

Beth Beede constructs one of her designs of fiber and feathers combined with glass.

MORNING SUN. Beth Beede. Fused glass colored with transparent yellow and orange glass powders. Nichrome wires, orange handmade beads and dyed top Merino sheep fleece are combined in the exotic wall sculpture. *Photo by Erik Redlich.*

strength window glass discs were fused together with laminated lengths of nichrome wire fanning out from near the center of the glass and extending beyond it. One of two additional smaller glass discs was divided into wedges with a glass cutter. The small full circle was coated with transparent glass enamel and the wedged sectons were sifted with orange to red orange toward the center. When the wedge-shaped sections had been fused to the small full circle, this assemblage was set out from the two fused large glass discs by a small piece of glass glued between them with G.E. Silicone Cement. Handmade orange

glass beads from Pakistan and fluffs of top Merino sheep fleece dyed yellow and orange were fastened into the ends of the extending wires that were twisted into loops.

For a fused glass and macramé suspension, identical large glass shapes were fused together with laminated transparent blue and turquoise glass enamels flowing into one another. Small air spaces made in the enamel and bits of baking soda form the planned bubbles. Silver wire loops for hangers were fused between the glass layers at their lower edge and a double wire twisted loop at the top for the macramé suspensions. The small

Sculptured wall pendant. Beth Beede. Two large single-strength window glass shapes with blues and turquoise glass ices and silver wire loops laminated between them. Bubbles are from tiny dots of baking soda. Smaller discs, laminated flashlight lenses, are colored with blue and turquoise glass powders. They are suspended on macrame cords of monofilament.

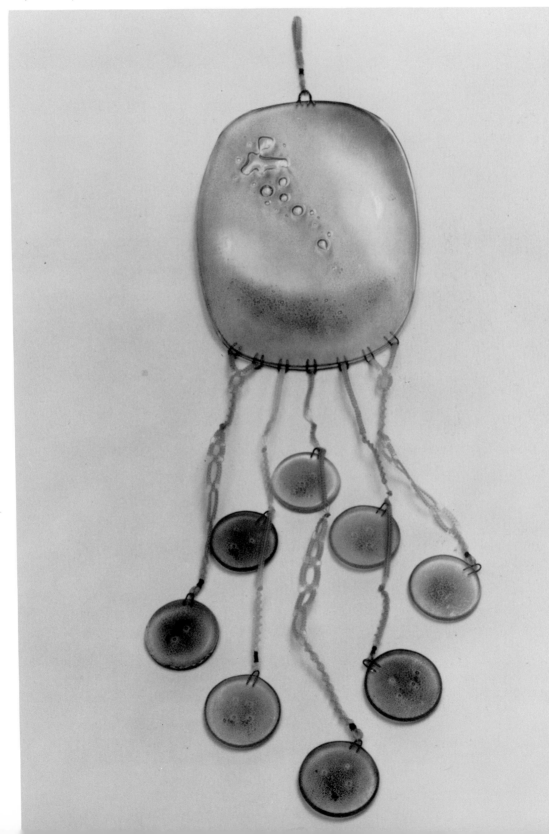

Detail of sculptured wall suspension.

suspended glass discs are made from fused flashlight lenses. They are in turquoise and blue hues, two each color. The bubbles were formed by the same method as those in the larger glass shape. Macramé done with monofilament (fishline) in blue and turquoise tints is finished with silver wire wound around the turned-up ends.

COPPER FOILING

Copper foil experimentation with segments of faceted glass, to make mobiles and sculptures, is creative and alluring. Sun streaming through these thick chunks of stained glass gives them a wondrous jewel-like glitter.

The copper foil is pliable and easy to use. To attain rigidity and durability once it has been applied to the glass segments, it must be coated with solder. Copper foil can be bought in ¼- and ⅜-inch rolls, 36 feet long, with an adhesive backing. If you want to use wider, less expensive copper foil that is nonadhesive, unroll it and cut off a strip about twenty inches long. Mark off ¼- or ⅜-inch intervals along each end of the strip. Lay a straightedge along a length of the foil and begin scoring with a nail or other scriber between marked intervals from one end of the strip to the other. With small sharp scissors, cut off *only a few* strips at one time along scored lines; if you cut too many at once they may tangle. Lay the strips on paper so they do not touch one another. Apply one of the new spray adhesives over the surface of a few strips. When the adhesive feels tacky but not sticky, it is time to begin applying the foil. The purpose of the adhesive is to hold the foil in place until it is soldered.

The copper foil applied in the demonstrated project is an adhesive-backed ¼-inch kind. The glass is broken faceted stained glass segments. Narrow ready-coated foil has paper backing that is peeled away as you apply the foil to a glass edge. You must keep foil and glass clean and free of oil from your skin; after it is cleaned, handle it gingerly. Alcohol or acetone will clean off oils.

To begin, pick up a clean glass piece, peel away some paper backing and wrap the foil along a glass ridge so an equal amount of foil is pressed to each side of the ridge. Press it firmly into all crevices and cut off the foil strip so it fits flush with the starting end. Apply soldering flux (oleic acid) to the ends of the copper strip and solder them together. If the solder does not cling to the copper, it may be soiled or the soldering iron may not be hot enough. Because the melting point of copper is much higher than that if tin or lead, there is little danger of melting the copper strip. Apply a few foil strips in different directions over the glass lump along its ridges, then cover the copper generously with 60/40 solid core solder to create a firm tight "cage" around the glass (Don't forget the soldering flux!). To suspend the glass as a mobile, solder an 18-gauge wire hanger to it. For exciting sculptures, solder foiled glass chunks together and epoxy them to a base.

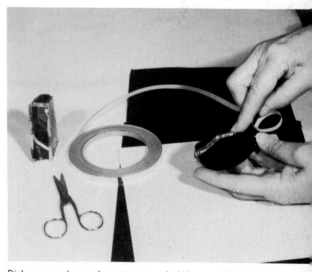

Pick up a clean glass piece as lightly as possible to keep skin oil from soiling it. Peel off some paper backing and press the narrow copper foil along a glass ridge.

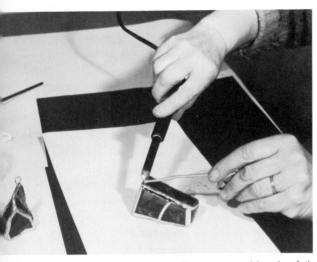

Press the foil firmly into all crevices; solder the foil ends together. Apply soldering flux and run solder over the entire copper foil area. Twisted wire hangers are soldered into place.

Small copper-foiled hanging sculptures made with dalle glass segments.

Faceted glass sculpture. Jean Abbott. Four three-dimensional stained glass pyramid shapes foiled and soldered together. 12" tall. *Photo by Alden Abbott.*

GLASS CASTING

Cast glass is an ancient art form dating back as far as the fifteenth century B.C. Shallow bowls, relief sculptures, and small figurines of remarkable detail have been found in ancient Egyptian tombs. The Egyptians valued small colored glass bits as highly as gemstones. Precious jeweled body ornaments from archaeological findings reveal handmade glass beads and small glass amulets. Glass casting continued intermittently throughout the southern Mediterranean area right up to the advent of blown glass around the first century A.D. Thereafter, the old method of casting glass seems to have been neglected until the beginning of the twentieth century, when Décorchemont, Rousseau, and other Frenchmen began to create sizable cast glass bowls and strong glass relief sculptures.

The formation of a small cast glass relief requires a model and a mold mixture that will be expendable after it is fired. The model for the relief can be made in either clay or wax. For the first basic sculptural relief project, the model is clay. Almost any clay will do, because it will not be fired. The small crucifix for the demonstration project is made from white sculpture clay, bought moist from the supplier. The model is placed flat on a sheet of glass or Formica-covered board; position the model with the front side facing up. Cut a strip of linoleum a little more than an inch wider than the deepest measurement of the clay model and several inches longer than its circumference. Wrap the strip around the model, smooth side facing inward and standing on edge; allow at least 1½ inches between the model and the linoleum. A string tied around the linoleum will hold it while you press clay all along the crack where the linoleum meets the sheet of glass or Formica board. Brush some vegetable oil or soap size over the inside of the linoleum strip and the base so the mold will release from it easily. The next step is to prepare the mold material.

The mold must be strong enough that it does not crack while it is being fired, but friable enough that it can be broken away from the glass object when it has been removed from the kiln. Most glass-casting molds today have a base of some form of plaster, combined with materials such as calcined refractory clay or silica sand and vermiculite or pulverized asbestos. The mold mixture developed especially for the demonstration project is made of equal parts of builder's plaster and a castable refractory powder called Plicast Verilite (trade name). This material is commonly used for commercial furnace linings. Kastolite is another satisfactory material. By consulting the telephone book classified advertisements, you may locate a local source of castable refractory material.

Blend thoroughly equal parts of dry plaster and the powdered material. Wear plastic gloves if you mix it by hand; plaster is very drying to the skin. Sprinkle the dry mixture over the surface of water in a plastic basin until it begins to pile up above the water just as though you were mixing plaster by itself. For one or two molds, two cups of water are sufficient for mixing adequate mold material. Be sure to add dry powder to water, not water to dry material. *Let it stand* for several minutes to slake or absorb, then blend it with a large wood or plastic spoon until it begins to thicken like heavy cream. Pour it immediately over the clay model in the prepared linoleum strip mold form to at least ¾ inch above the clay model. The mix will seem thin at first, but it will thicken and set in ten to twenty minutes. After it sets about an hour, the linoleum can be removed and soon the clay model is pulled from the mold. See that every bit of clay is removed from the mold and bevel the edges carefully. The mold is very fragile until its preliminary firing, so handle it gingerly. The inside of the mold cavity is painted with a thin solution of kiln wash for a separator. Set the completed mold in a warm place to dry for 24 hours. In the meantime completely scrub the plastic basin and tools used to mix and form the mold. If they are not cleaned at once, it is difficult to remove residue of mold material. After the fresh mold dries for 24 hours, set it into a cool kiln with the door or lid cracked ½ inch and turn switches to *low*. Fire it slowly to 400°–500°F to remove gases from the plaster that could cloud the glass. *When the kiln cools,* remove the mold with care.

For the demonstration piece, small fragments of washed antique glass were carefully positioned in the mold. Avoid scratching the mold cavity lining so bits of plaster or kiln wash (with which the lining is painted) are not mingled with glass particles. The filled mold was set gingerly into the kiln and fired until it reached 1650°F. The glass was cooled and annealed for 4 hours. Tests made for this project suggested that in certain colorless sheet glasses, devitrification (crystallization) tended to occur just *below* the temperature of liquefication if held there for a protracted period of time. When the rate of rise or descent was increased between 1650°F and 1450°F, crystallization did not occur. It did not occur when stained glass was used. Window glass has a higher liquefication temperature than stained glass.

When the glass was annealed and cooled, the casting was removed and the mold was broken away from it. After the glass sculpture was scrubbed with a stiff brush and water to clean off bits of kiln wash and mold material clinging to it, roughness around the edge was stoned smooth under water with a fine carborundum stone. The sculpture was dried and cemented to a section of granite rock with epoxy resin.

Preparation is made for casting molds; a large mold will be made for casting a glass cross and two smaller molds for glass draping. It is practical to make more than one mold at a time when the mixture is made up.

After the mold has set for an hour or more, the linoleum strip and clay model are removed from it. The clay is dug out easily with a loop end modeling tool.

Paint the mold's interior with a solution of kiln wash. Handle the fragile mold with care until it dries.

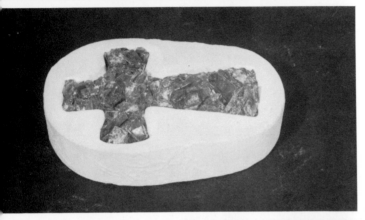

Small chunks of antique dalle glass fill the mold to rounding. The level will sink as the glass liquefies.

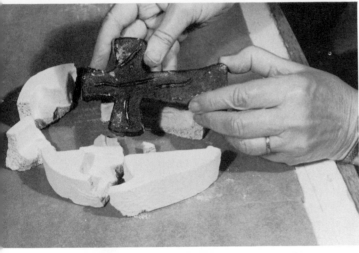

After the casting is fired, annealed, and cooled, break away the mold and scrub off the residue of kiln wash.

Cast glass cross. Polly Rothenberg. Deep ruby red antique glass mounted on natural unpolished red granite.

Regardless of how smooth the inside surface of a casting mold may be, the surface of a cast glass form takes on a slight graininess from the mold lining. You may prefer a more highly reflective surface for your cast glass. Although the procedure of fire-polishing rough glass is not usually available to the average individual craftsman, another method can be employed. Clean the glass with detergent water and dry it. Wipe a *thin* film of squeegee oil or other enameling oil over it, or spray it with enameling gum. Sift a very thin coating of low-firing glass flux over all but the back surface of the glass and dry it in a warm place. Fire it again *slowly,* back side down, following regular firing procedures to the temperature at which the flux is shiny. Vent the kiln from time to time if the temperature rises too rapidly. Be sure to anneal it as it cools! Because of the thickness of cast glass, reheating, cooling, and annealing *must be slow enough* to prevent the glass from cracking. Specific timing is not given due to variations in kilns and glasses.

EDRIS ECKHARDT'S SCULPTURES

Edris Eckhardt, talented ceramic and glass sculptor, combines glass casting with fusing and lamination for her sensitive sculptures. Her cast glass is formed in the lost-wax process; she formulates her own glasses with special oxide colorants and casts them in compatible investment molds.

STRANGE BLOSSOM. Edris Eckhardt. The preformed glass was inserted in the wax model to be cast in bronze. High temperature glass to withstand 2300°F bronze when the metal was cast. Colors: metal, golden bronze to dark brown; glass, iridescent. Mounted on black marble. Photo by Ray Sommer.

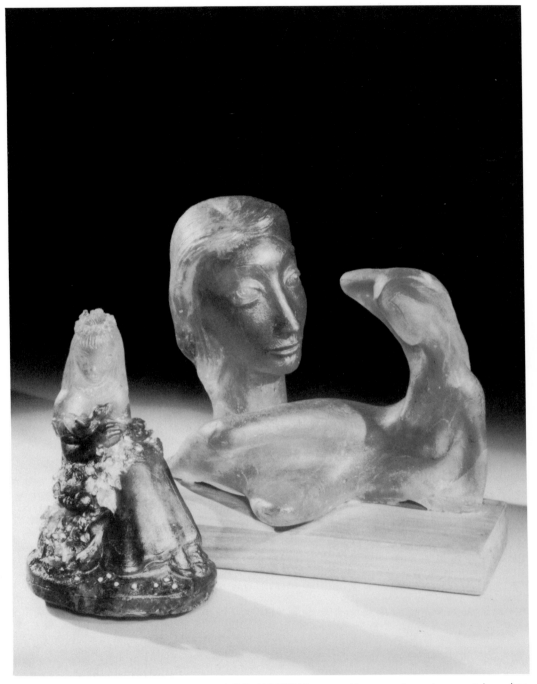

Cast glass group. Edris Eckhardt. *Left:* JUNE MORNING, emerald green, turquoise, crystal, amber, chartreuse. Head, SUMMER, peach color glass. NUDE, pink. All pieces from Edris's retrospective exhibition at the Corning Glass Museum. *Photo courtesy The Corning Museum of Glass.*

CHERUBIM. Edris Eckhardt. Low relief. Glass fused into investment. Colors: jade green, semiopaque. Transparent gold over raised surfaces.

◀

AND THOU BESIDE ME. Edris Eckhardt. Relief panel mounted for indirect light. Glass fused into investment material. Colors: emerald, turquoise, chartreuse with transparent gold over all raised surfaces.

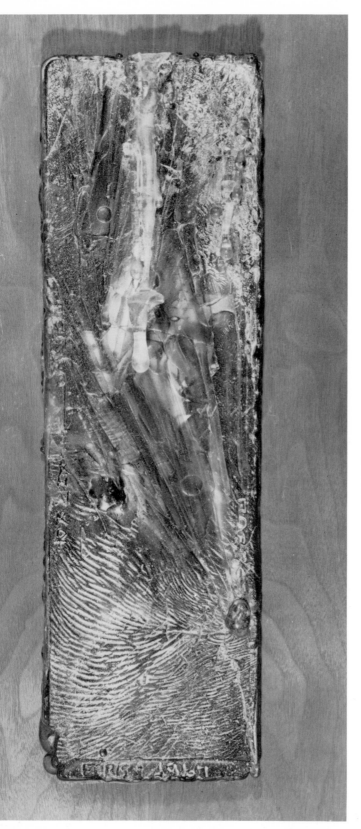

THE SOURCE. Edris Eckhardt. The story of water from a drop to the Delta. Illuminated low-relief sculpture. Made of fused laminated glass. Colors: emerald and moss greens, cobalt and turquoise blues, pink and crystal white. Edris Eckhardt is an eminent sculptor who works in several mediums. She makes all her own glass, from the sands to the coloring oxides. *Photo courtesy The Corning Museum of Glass.*

▶

Cast and fused glass squares set into fences. At the Blenko Glass Company Visitors Center, Milton, West Virginia.

BLENKO GLASS

Fused and Cast Glass Fences at The Blenko Glass Company Visitors Center.

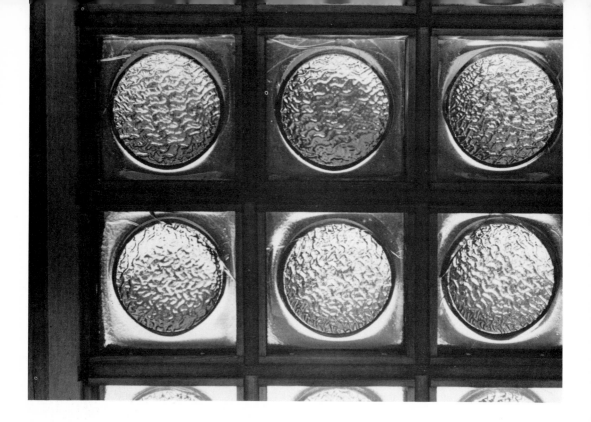

GLASSART STUDIO'S CALIFORNIA MART SKYLIGHT

The Glassart Studio of America in Phoenix, Arizona, completed in 1973 the magnificent 2,200-square-foot faceted stained glass skylight of the California Mart in Los Angeles. It is the largest single stained glass skylight in the United States: 65 feet long, 35 feet wide, with 126 panels that are 2 feet by 7 feet.

Faceted stained glass skylight at the California Mart, in Los Angeles. Completed by Glassart Studio, Phoenix, Arizona, in 1973. The skylight contains over 2,200 square feet; 65 feet long, 35 feet wide; 126 panels, each 2 feet by 7 feet. *Photo by courtesy of Glassart Studio.*

Top of the faceted glass skylight at California Mart as it appears from four stories above. One vertical side of the skylight can be seen along the right edge.

View from beneath the California Mart skylight. The sides of the skylight can be seen.

Detail of the skylight from below center.

Detail of the skylight design from below the portion near one end. See color plate. *Photos of the California Mart faceted stained glass skylight by courtesy of Glassart Studio.*

One of twelve windows in Saint Ambrose Catholic Church, Salt Lake City, Utah. Glassart Studio. A combination of faceted stained glass dalles and leaded glass in concrete.

Leaded stained glass window in Paradise Valley Methodist Church, Phoenix, Arizona. Glassart Studio.

Close view of Paradise Valley Methodist
Church window.

Distinctive faceted stained glass skylight
in a residential home. Glassart Studio.

Leaded stained glass residential bathroom window. Glassart Studio.

Faceted stained glass residential door. Glassart Studio.

Leaded stained glass arched window. Glassart Studio.

Faceted stained glass doorside panel. Glassart Studio.

◀

Clerestory windows of faceted stained glass. Glassart Studio. Eliminates the need for draperies above doors leading to an Arcadia patio.

EDWARD J. BYRNE STUDIO

Edward Byrne glazes (leads) etched glass panels.

Upper right:
Lead camed window with metallic overlay. Edward J. Byrne Studio.

Detail of camed window with overlay.

THE CUMMINGS ARCHITECTURAL WINDOW

"The window is 36 feet by 13 feet and the sill is 11 feet off the ground. The photograph shows only five of the six sections. . . . It is in the Officers' Open Mess, Fort Lewis, Washington. The problem to solve: 'A stained glass window to hide the brick wall outside . . .' well, look! In the final analysis, the brick wall became an integral visual part of the window; lights are projected on the brick wall at night to add a third dimension to the window. Another problem was that there is clear plate glass, glazed into each of the six sections, that was there to stay. Our window was to be placed on the inside of the plate glass at a distance of 6 inches; in order to avoid problems of condensation, we built our window with holes in it. The black areas are not glass at all, but black acrylic . . . The areas that appear as gray in the photo are a commercially made stained glass called 'Pentacore' by Mississippi Glass. The clear areas are the 'holes' in our window. They allow for plenty of air circulation so there will never be any problem of moisture buildup between the two windows. Lastly, the 'leads' are not leads at all, but are 1¾-inch bronze anodized aluminum with snapon beads." —Judy Cummings.

A window beautifully planned to cope with a major architectural problem. Designed by Hilda Sachs and H. M. Cummings. Executed by Cummings Studio, San Rafael, California, for the Officers' Open Mess, Fort Lewis, Washington.

FARBIGEM AND THE WILLETS

"Exploration on the part of several stained glass studios, both American and European, into the possibility of locating colored glass works of art in commercial buildings and homes, necessitated moving away from leaded glass of the medieval style found in traditional churches and cathedrals. This lead to a certain amount of experimentation with new techniques.

"A most revolutionary method of using glass as an art form was originated in Holland by Florin Van Tetterode. His striking installations in banks, hotels, shops, and office buildings came to the attention of Mr. and Mrs. Henry Lee Willet in 1965. An arrangement was soon made whereby they would have exclusive rights to the process in the United States . . . At the Willet Stained Glass Studios it was given the name Farbigem.

"Farbigem is a technique making possible an art form in which whole walls can be designed in decorative thicknesses of glass. Starting with a base of two thicknesses of plate glass with plexiglass between, areas of colored glasses and/or masses of clear crystal can be laminated layer on layer on either or both sides. The permanence and safety of the resulting sculptured effect, in spite of its great weight, is assured through the use of special adhesives.

"The medium is especially successful in nonrepresentational abstract designs, although the two panels telling the history of medicine in the Ohio State University Medical Center are full of accurate portraits. The versatility of Farbigem is evident. It is used for small freestanding sculptures, gigantic three-dimensional effects on exterior facades as well as in window walls and room dividers. It has been successfully combined with faceted glass and sandblasted glass. It is effective with either a daylight or artificial light source from the back, and also when surface lighted."—Helene Weis.

The Willets' splendid Ohio State University Medical Center Farbigem murals depict great milestones in the advance of medicine around the world and medical services to humanity. Bonded layers of flat glass set vertically, varicolored spheres, cylinders, faceted chunks, and gemmaux backgrounds, together with heads, lettering, and other special representations acid-etched on flashed glass, create an aesthetic effect of scintillating imagery and storytelling.

WORLD HISTORY OF MEDICINE. Willet Studio. Designed for and installed in Ohio State University Medical Center, Columbus, Ohio. Illuminated Farbigem glass wall. Bonded in layers of colored stained glass and clear glass.

▶

Finished Farbigem for Ohio State University. Close view showing depth and laminated textures.

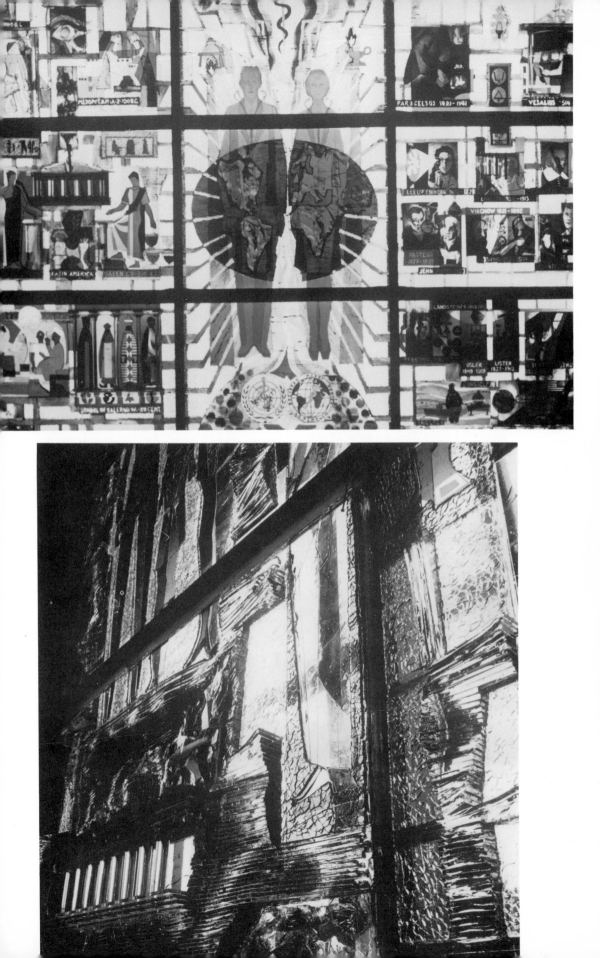

Detail of Ohio State University glass mural with its intricate layering and texture.

Additional detail of Ohio State University Farbigem mural.

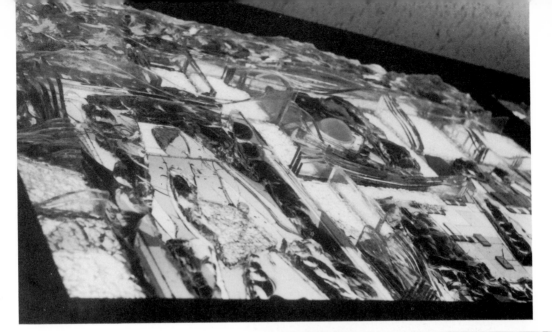

View from beneath the Ohio State Farbigem freestanding mural showing intricate variety and depth of individual applications.

Farbigem panel on a bank building in Dordrecht, Holland, executed by Van Tetterode's Studio, Amsterdam, Holland.

Many skilled glassworkers are required to plan and construct one of these truly heroic compositions. Vincent Sirrianni of the Willet Studios lays out glass for the Farbigem mural in Ohio State
University Medical Center.

Edgar Williams prepares glass for lamination of the mural wall at the Willet Studios.

Detail of the Farbigem Teilhard de Chardin window in Riverside Park Methodist Church, Jacksonville, Florida. Made by Willet Stained Glass Studios.

TABLETS OF THE LAW. Willet Stained Glass Studios. Bonding in the Farbigem process can be combined with any other glass method. It is combined here with faceted glass. Greenborough Hebrew Congregation, Dobbs Ferry, New York.

The Willet Stained Glass Studios has an illustrious experience in faceted glass applications as well as in Farbigem. Henry Willet selects glass dalles for a faceted window.

Marguerite Gaudin designs a black and white for a faceted lumiere. Willet Stained Glass Studios.

Donald Consul selects and knobs dalles for a faceted window at Willet Stained Glass Studios.

Phillip Tate faceting stained glass dalles at Willet's.

Willet Studio personnel installing a faceted window in the Zion Lutheran Church, Anaheim, California.

St. Mark's Episcopal Church, New Canaan, Connecticut. The interior of the church and faceted windows, both by Willet Stained Glass Studios.

Glossary

Annealing Glass: The heating and controlled cooling of glass to relieve stress and brittleness. The temperature range for annealing varies, depending on characteristics of the glass.

Antique Glass: Sheets of stained glass made by blowing.

Batch: Glass ingredients put into a furnace to be melted.

Bending: Softening and sagging of glass during kiln-firing.

Blank: A piece of glass cut to basic shape for use in creating a bent glass object.

Blocking: Shaping a gather or bubble of glass with a wooden block or other object.

Blown Glass: Glass objects that have been formed by blowing air into a gather of molten glass. The resultant glass bubble is shaped into many forms.

Blowpipe: An iron or steel pipe with a nose of heatproof alloy for gathering molten glass from a furnace. Air is blown through the pipe to inflate the gather into a glass bubble.

Bonded Glass: Pieces of glass cemented together or to a glass sheet with transparent adhesive.

Bridge: A flat wooden strip elevated with end blocks to support the hand while it is painting glass over a light table.

Bridge Wall: A wall across the top section of a tank beneath which molten glass flows, to trap impurities.

Bubble: 1. Air pocket trapped in glass when it is fused. 2. The large pocket of air intentionally formed when glass is blown.

Calcine: To heat inorganic substances to a high temperature (without fusion) to pulverize or oxidize.

Calcium Carbonate: Whiting. A separating powder used between glass and molds or kiln shelves to prevent adhesion when fired.

Came: Lead strips that join pieces of stained glass.

Carborundum Stone: A silicon carbide stone for hand-grinding rough spots on glass. Should be done under water.

Cartoon: The layout design of a stained glass composition in actual size.

Cathedral Glass: Machine-rolled stained glass with medium to heavy texture on one side and a smooth surface on the other side, 1/8-inch thickness uniformly.

Caulk: To stop up seams and make them watertight.

Coefficient of Expansion: The rate at which glass (or other material) expands during heating and contracts during cooling.

Collage: An assemblage of fragments of glass to create an art composition.

Conchoidal: Having swirled elevations and depressions in form, such as one-half of a conch shell.

Contoured: Glass sagged or slumped over a mold in the kiln to bend it to the shape of the mold.

Crazing: A mesh of fine cracks in glass caused by too rapid or imperfect cooling.

Cullet: Broken or refuse glass usually added to new material to facilitate melting of a glass batch in a furnace.

Curious Glass: Fragments of sheet glass sold as scrap glass.

Cut-size Line: Cutline. The border line of the stained glass composition against which the border lead will be placed.

Cutting: A term often used for scoring and separating glass; the glass is not actually cut.

Dalles: From the French *dalles* [doll] *de verre* (flagstones of glass). Slabs of antique stained glass measuring 3/4 inch to 2 inches in thickness. Usually cast in squares or rectangles with dimensions of 8 inches to 12 inches.

Embossed: Surface with raised designs.

Etching: Chemical or mechanical erosion of surface to make designs.

Faceted Glass: Slab glass chipped to produce sparkling light-reflective small planes in a conchoidal fracture.

Ferrier's Nails: Horseshoe nails for securing glass and leads together; blue lath nails are often substituted.

Fine Silver: Pure silver. Does not oxidize when it is fired.

Firebrick: A hard refractory brick with extremely high heat resistance. Not to be confused with insulation brick.

Flashed Stained Glass: Denotes a variety of antique, having a light-colored glass base with thinner skins of richer, deeper contrasting colored glass.

Flux: 1. Colorless glass ground to fine mesh. 2. A substance for promoting fusion in soldering. See Oleic Acid.

Foil: An extra-thin metal sheeting.

Fracture: Breaking or splitting and cracking of glass.

Fusing: Combining glass pieces through heat by melting together.

Gather: The molten glass picked up on the end of the blowpipe from the hot furnace melt.

Gemmaux: An application of many small colored glass chunks and bits bonded together for a scintillating effect.

Glass Cutter: A small hand-held steel or wood-handled tool with a tiny cutting wheel set into one end. The tool is used to score glass so it can be separated or cleanly broken apart. Some cutters have minute commercial diamonds instead of steel wheels.

Glazier: A craftsman who sets glass and putties its edges to weatherproof it.

Glazing: Enclosing window openings or other areas with glass by puttying, cementing, leading.

Glazing Compound: Putty used to secure glass in a leaded composition.

Glory Hole: A furnace for reheating glass on a rod or punty when blowing glass.

Greenware: Unfired bone-dry ceramic objects sold by ceramic suppliers. They can often be fired for use as glass bending molds if they have no undercuts.

Grout: A creamy mortar filled in between ceramic or glass tiles.

Grozing: Chipping away irregular projections to refine the edge or to improve the fit of glass.

Halation: The spread of light beyond the boundaries of a lighted object to create a diffused ring or imagery of light or color on adjoining objects.

Heart: The thin crossbar between channels of lead came.

H-lead: H-shaped double channeled lead came.

Hardener: One of two components in epoxy resin. It causes the hardening of the resin.

Ices or Ice Colors: Colored glass powder used for decorating glass surfaces when they are fired.

Impervious: Impenetrable or unaffected by moisture, light rays, chemicals, etc.

Incise: To cut.

Insulation Brick: A soft porous brick with high heat resistance; may be carved to make glass-bending molds. Sometimes incorrectly called firebrick.

Jack: A steel or waxed wood two-pronged spring tool for shaping molten glass that is being formed.

Jewels: Small lumps of colored glass that have been fired and then adhered to glass objects for decoration.

Kastolite: Brand name. A castable refractory sometimes used for making molds to be used for glass bending. Its primary use is for furnace lining.

Kiln: A high temperature oven, ideally equipped with a pyrometer, used for firing glass, enamels, clay, and refractory molds.

Kiln Wash: Equal parts of kaolin and flint in powdered form or creamy solution.

Lamination: Two or more glass pieces fused flat or bent together with materials entrapped between them.

Lath Nails: Small thin hard carpenter's nails that may be employed to hold glass and leads together during construction of a stained glass composition.

Lathekin: A small smooth bluntly pointed or almond shaped tool for opening the channels of lead came.

Lavender Oil: An oil derived from the lavender plant. It can be used as a binder for application of enamels.

Leading: Joining pieces of stained glass together with lead came strips.

Lehr: An oven designed for annealing stained glass.

Light Table: An enclosure with frosted glass (ground glass) top through which artificial light is transmitted.

Lumiere: A design in color for a stained glass window.

Luster: A metallic overglaze.

Marver: A steel or marble-topped table on which a molten glass gather is rolled and cooled slightly.

Matrix: The base in which another form is developed. In a faceted glass panel, the cement or epoxy surrounding each glass segment is the matrix.

Matting: Applying glass paint to a glass surface, then tapping it with a badger brush to give a translucent surface.

Maturity: The temperature at which fired glass attains its full beauty.

Mica: A fireproof silicate that separates into thin sheets.

Nichrome: An acid-resistant refractory alloy of nickel, iron, and chromium.

Oleic Acid: A fatty oil used for a flux in soldering lead.

Opalescent Glass: Milky semitranslucent rolled glass in one or more swirled colors and white. It is somewhat brittle and is difficult to cut.

Oxidize: To combine chemically with oxygen. Metals, when weathered, darken or change color by oxidation.

Punty: A slender steel rod for picking up extra bits of molten glass to decorate a blown form or to attach to the base of the form so the blowpipe can be removed. Also called pontil rod.

Pyrometer: An instrument for measuring and indicating kiln temperatures.

Refractory: Hard and resistant to high temperatures.

Release Agent: A separator for preventing glass or mold material from adhering to one another.

Repoussé: A hammered, pressed, or raised design in metals.

Rheostat: Device for regulating electric current temperatures by variable controls.

Resin Core Solder: Solder with an invisible resin core that does not require flux. Not suitable for leaded glass.

Rondel: Round disc of stained antique glass.

Sagging: Loss of rigidity as fired glass slumps into the shape of its supporting mold.

Sandblasting: Engraving with a high-velocity stream of sand on areas not protected by tape to create surface patterns.

Seedy Glass: Contains tiny bubbles that create a texture.

Sgraffito: Designs created by scratching into enamel or glaze before firing.

Shard: A fragment of a brittle substance such as glass or pottery.

Shears, Cartoon: Scissors for cutting out individual stained glass patterns. They have a single-edged blade and a double-edged blade. When a cut is made, the blades remove a strip of paper between pattern pieces to make room for the lead heart that separates glass pieces.

Slab Glass: Clear colored antique glass cast in thick slabs used for facet glass.

Soldering: Joining metals with solder by heating with a soldering iron.

Square Shears: When they close, the shears form a square hole for cutting or clasping molten glass rods or gobs.

Stained Glass: Glass colored with oxides and other chemicals incorporated into the batch while it is molten.

Stencil: A design pattern around which colors are sifted or painted to transfer the design to glass or other surfaces.

Stopping Knife: A short-bladed knife with a rounded bent end. Useful for lifting and inserting glass shapes into lead channels.

Strain Point: The lower limit of the annealing range, which varies with the type of glass being annealed.

Stress: Inner strain of glass caused by improper annealing or by fusing incompatible glasses together.

Striations: Random threadlike lines or grooves in surfaces of glass.

Subsurface: The bottom side of a piece of glass.

Temperature Gradient: The uniform or graded rate of rising or lowering of temperature.

Template: A pattern cut from thin material to an exact shape.

Tesserae: Glass cut into small pieces for making mosaics.

Tinning: Coating the copper tip of a soldering iron with tin-lead solder.

Translucent: Diffused transmission of light rays.

Transmitted Light: Light that passes through glass or other material.

Transparent: Full transmission of light rays with clear vision of objects through the glass.

Undercut: A cut that slants inward, preventing bent or cast glass from releasing from its mold.

U-lead: Single channeled U-shaped lead came, used especially for border leading.

Vent: An opening to permit passage of heat,

Index